HANCOCK'S LAST STAND

HANCOCK'S LAST STAND

The Series That Never Was

Edward Joffe

The Book Guild Ltd
Sussex, England

The Book Guild Ltd
25 High Street,
Lewes, Sussex

First published 1998
© Edward Joffe, 1998

Set in Times
Typesetting by Keyboard Services, Luton, Bedfordshire

Printed in Great Britain by
Bookcraft (Bath) Ltd, Avon

A catalogue record for this book is
available from the British Library

ISBN 1 85776 316 5

For my children Lynn, Layne, Steven and Victoria; my siblings Justin and Amelia; and in memory of my parents Rita and Harry.

CONTENTS

FOREWORD

Is he as funny 'off' as he is 'on' is a question you are constantly being asked if you work with comics. I have been privileged to work with quite a few and, on the whole, the answer is 'no!' There are exceptions of course, but Tony was not one of those few.

I first worked with him on a Rediffusion series for Jack Hylton in 1956 and, even then, he was a worrier – would it be alright ... shouldn't he be doing something more worthy of his talents – was it funny enough? I don't think he ever appreciated just how much fun and laughter he brought to so many people's lives via television, radio and the theatre.

In 1961 came 'The Blood Donor', a magnificently conceived and written half-hour by Ray Galton and Alan Simpson, and possibly Tony's best ever performance, in spite of the fact that he was using Autocue, which in those days was to the side of the camera and drew his eyes away from the person he was talking to!

I certainly don't recall Tony ever being under the influence during a recording, though he certainly enjoyed a glass or two after the show.

Some years later, when I was in his television series set in a nightclub, he was starting to go downhill, and it was very sad to see such a talent being wasted.

Edward Joffe has written a truthful, loving and heart-rending account of Tony's last months in Australia. There are many amusing moments among the agonising ones in this story of a very unhappy comic.

June Whitfield, 1998

ACKNOWLEDGEMENTS

Special thanks:
To Joan Le Mesurier and Clare Wales for their generosity in allowing me to quote from treasured personal letters and, in Joan's case, from her book *Lady Don't Fall Backwards* and from John's *A Jobbing Actor*. To them, and to Merlyn and Lindy for awakening dormant memory banks. To Jussie for his unflagging support, encouragement and analytical eye. To Arnie Gordon, my cheerleader. And, by no means least, to Carol Biss with gratitude for her faith in the project.

*   *   *

This book could not have been completed without the invaluable assistance of a lot of lovely people who were exceptionally liberal with their time, their memories, their hospitality, their opinions, their talent, their friendship and their permissions... Each will know which categories are theirs. Thank you all. Alphabetically, of course!

Hugh Alexander, Malcolm Chapman, Russell Clark, Oliver Cyriax, George Fairweather, Liz Fraser, Catherine Freeman, Ray Galton, Nigel Grant, Kenneth Griffith, Damaris Hayman, Stephanie Kaye, Jon Mangan, Lawrie Masterson, Allan Mewton, Philip Oakes, Dan Peat & the Tony Hancock Appreciation Society, Pacific Publications – Melbourne, Phyllis Rounce, Dave Sandall and the Tony

Hancock Society, Seven Network – Australia, Mike Sharland, Alan Simpson, Hugh Stuckey, Beryl Vertue, all the HANCOCK crew and cast in Oz, and others too numerous to mention who checked important details or helped trace key people with whom I'd lost contact.

BY WAY OF INTRODUCTION

What I have written is not an intellectual assessment of the Hancock psyche. I am not qualified to do that. It is merely the story of a great talent's last months on earth, with personal opinions from people who were there at the time or knew him, plus warts and all observations of a man in turmoil – a man battling with alcoholism. I hope this document will provide a clearer picture and perhaps a better understanding of a people's Pagliaccio, one of the finest entertainers Britain has ever produced.

This book has been in and out of my mind for a long time. I've often been questioned about my association with Tony Hancock as his last director, and on each occasion I felt I must get round to committing it to paper. Fortunately, I've been too busy.

The final, decisive inspiration for starting this book is due to Phyllis Rounce, who was Tony Hancock's first agent – and mine – since she it was who offered me the opportunity to work with Tony Hancock in Australia, where I inevitably became part of his life and his legend. She it was who caused me to be at the THAS – the Tony Hancock Appreciation Society – annual dinner and convention in Bournemouth, held at Tony Hancock's parents' former hotel, where I met a dedicated band of Hancock enthusiasts, many of whom were toddlers, or unborn, when Tony Hancock was the brightest star on British television in the Fifties.

THAS invited me to attend their dinner – a sort of Hancockian

Burns Night complete with videos of some of his commercials, excerpts from his movies and his classic television programmes. All I had to do in return for a quite splendid night out was to answer a few questions from members about my experiences with Hancock in Australia. This inspired me to dig into a mouldy storage box of documents, mementos, photographs, scripts, and yellowing, long-forgotten letters.

Among the contents of that box was correspondence to and from my family, Tony's mother, my agent, and others, as well as production memoranda, art department drawings, floor plans, notes, news cuttings galore and other bits and bobs dating back more than a quarter of a century.

I rediscovered some unique, unpublished photographs and 90 colour transparencies. When I spoke to friends, members of my family and people who had known Tony well or had worked with him, many were kind enough to share with me their verbal or written recollections of the way things were in Hancock's Australia in the first half of 1968.

1

'How would you like to work
with Tony Hancock?'

In the days before they chirruped like constipated crickets, my telephone rang.

'How would you like to work with Tony Hancock?'

Silence.

'Hello, hello? Are you there?' asked the voice at the other end.

'Yes, yes, I'm here,' I said, 'only I thought you said how would you like to work with Tony Hancock.'

'I did say that.'

'OK Phyllis,' I laughed, 'pull the other one, it's got bells on.'

'I'm serious,' said Phyllis Rounce.

Phyllis Rounce was Hancock's first agent. During the war she had served her country in AWS2*, the army's entertainment unit. When peace broke out, she and her army boss, Colonel Bill Alexander, decided that since they knew most of the acts who had entertained the troops they would start a talent agency, which they modestly christened International Artistes Representation.

Phyllis' primary role in the venture was talent-spotting, and she was one of the few women to regularly visit the famous 'We

---

* AWS2 – Army Welfare Services – Entertainment. Less well-known than the high-profile ENSA, which entertained all the services – Army, Air Force and Navy. ENSA is the acronym for Entertainment National Services Association – facetiously renowned among all servicemen and women as Every Night Something Awful!

Never Closed' Windmill Theatre in Soho, which featured nude ladies in 'tasteful' poses loosely inspired by classic works of art by Old Masters and mythology of dubious origin. The Lord Chamberlain had decreed that the girls were not allowed to move in front of the audience, so, to allow time to reset the deep-frozen tableaux in which the only detectable sign of life was the occasional blinking eyelid, comedians entertained the raincoat brigade, or, as Tony described them to Gareth Powell of *Chance* magazine: 'That unfortunate group of gentlemen with copies of the racing papers and U-boat Commanders' binoculars,' who wished to be titillated by the naked, frequently goosepimpled, ladies Tony called 'Little scrubbers with small tits like dartboards.' Needless to say, comedians didn't often garner the laughs they craved, as the audience came for a different craving which certainly did not include listening to gags, no matter how funny the comics happened to be.

Many of the best comedians of postwar Britain received their first dose of audience rejection at the Windmill. People like Peter Sellers, Jimmy Edwards, Harry Secombe, Bruce Forsyth, Dick Emery, Alfred Marks, Michael Bentine and Arthur Haynes, to drop but a few names, kept the wolf from the door with meagre Windmill pay packets of around £25 a week for six shows a day, six days a week. Hancock was one of them, and he lasted a lot longer than the three-night stand of double act Bartholomew and Wiseman, who would doubtless not have been a jot less popular if they hadn't changed their name to Morecambe and Wise.

Norman Wisdom, Spike Milligan, Roy Castle and Benny Hill weren't even granted auditions by 'VD', as the famous 'star-maker' Vivian Van Damm preferred to be called.

Tony was thrilled with his job at t'mill and wrote to all his friends to come and see him. 'A London newspaper even printed my name,' he recorded in the *Sunday Dispatch*, 'I hoped that Val Parnell or Jack Hylton would drop in and sign me up...' Parnell and Hylton were major impresarios, influential and powerful.

'When at last a charming thing called Phyllis Rounce dropped in and said she was pleasantly surprised to hear people laughing at the Windmill, and that I was indeed a funny man, I just said, "Well, that lot only come to see Gladys starkers. It's the hardest job in the world getting a laugh out of tired men who've been queueing in the rain since 10.30, with newspapers over their heads..."

'"Yes, I understand," she said. "That's why I wanted to talk to you about a contract."

'Only then did I discover that I *had* been discovered, and that I was talking to the representative of International Artistes, the big agents.'

The agency was responsible for shaping the careers of many a star performer, and Phyllis, herself a legend in her own lifetime, had been mother, sister, mentor, agent and friend to David Nixon, Rolf Harris, and Charlie Drake among others, but top of the list was Terry-Thomas, to whom Phyllis had presented the cigarette holder which became as well known a trademark as T-T's gap-toothed smile.

Phyllis had decided that Tony had what she was an expert at finding – star quality – and she offered to put him and his 'comedy duo' partner Derek Scott on the books of her fledgling agency. And a star was born. On 14 September 1948, Tony and Derek were auditioned by the BBC at the Star Sound Studios in Baker Street. On 1 November 1948 they appeared on a television programme called *New To You*. The rest, as they say, is showbiz history.

When asked what qualities she saw in the young Hancock, Phyllis says: 'The feet. The feet got everybody. He had wonderful feet. Nobody in the world had feet like that. Tony had his own special walk. His feet didn't always seem to belong to him, and he shambled along in the most amazing and amusing way. Yes, it was his feet that decided me to sign him up.'

Whether or not it was Tony's feet that appealed to the Great British Public, it wasn't long before Tony Hancock became the agency's most important, and unquestionably most demanding, client. He took to telephoning Phyllis at all hours of the day or night – a habit the writers and I were to discover for ourselves in Australia.

3

Apart from looking after his bookings and contracts, Phyllis' other duties included making sure that Tony reached his venues on time, that he had digs, transport, food and money in his pocket. She happily described her job as that of a glorified nursemaid, tending to all his creature comforts.

Eventually, as he had done previously, and would continue to do with other professional colleagues, Tony ditched Phyllis. Orders were left at the stage door of the Adelphi not to allow her backstage access. When she insisted on seeing him, he grudgingly deigned to admit her, but petulantly refused to speak to her. Thus, after five years of dedication to nurturing his burgeoning career and catering to his every need he dropped International Artistes without so much as a thank you or even a goodbye. But it was Phyllis Rounce who came to Tony's rescue 12 years later in connection with his Australian series.

At around the time he 'fired' Phyllis, he became involved with Freda (Freddie) Ross, who worked in public relations as Tony's publicist. She then became his mistress, his sparring partner and, finally, his second wife.

By 1967, when he was offered the Australian gig, Tony and Freddie were embroiled in vitriolic divorce proceedings, and Tony's last agent, Billy Marsh, had despaired of ever getting him any more work since his formidable drinking habits were, by then, so notorious in 'the business' that no one would touch him.

When Tony signed up for Australia, he insisted on a UK director. The Australian promoter John Collins, asked Jack Neary, a Sydney agent, to help find a suitable director. Jack Neary, who represented International Artistes in Australia, was aware that Tony's track record would preclude 'name' directors, so he contacted Phyllis Rounce.

I'd known Phyllis for a number of years and should have realised that she wouldn't joke about anything as important as giving Tony Hancock a leg back up onto the ladder of success. She still loved and admired the guy, despite the fact that she had lavished so much care, attention, time and effort on him and had devoted herself almost exclusively to promoting him and his career, only to have him spurn her totally.

4

She hadn't heard a dickey bird from Tony for ten years after he gave International Artistes the Order of the Boot until he rang her at 4 a.m. one morning to ask for the telephone number of some of her writers, who he wanted to work for him.

Phyllis Rounce put it this way: 'He was absolutely horrendous to people, but everybody forgave him. Women particularly wanted to mother him because they felt he was so vulnerable.' Phyllis herself was the uncrowned queen of this category and, still wanting to see Tony back on the top perch, she embarked on a search for a director.

In the Sixties there were very few freelance television directors about, and I was probably offered the job because there wasn't exactly a queue of them lining up to work with Tony Hancock. Other directors must have been approached before me. Many years later I learnt that Tony's former BBC TV producer, Duncan Wood, had turned it down flat. I don't know who else was asked, Phyllis having been too discreet to tell me. I may well have been her last hope.

I'd always been a Hancock fan. So much so that I never arranged outings on evenings when Tony's BBC television shows were being transmitted. I invariably nipped home early to catch them. It seemed to me that everyone else had the same idea because in Battersea, where I lived at the time, the evening traffic was generally very heavy, but if you looked out of the window on Friday nights when Tony's series was on air, there were far fewer vehicles about than on any other night of the week.

Tony Hancock was, arguably, the only solo comedian in the country who people really loved. Tommy Cooper, Max Wall, Frankie Howerd, Arthur Askey and many of Tony's other contemporaries were indeed often very funny, versatile, talented and popular, but with comedians, there's no halfway mark. Like 'em or loathe 'em. I cannot recall anyone who didn't like Hancock as a comedian. A few people couldn't stand him as a man, but even so, without exception, his peers were unstinting in their praise of his unique, often breathtaking, comedic talent.

When Phyllis Rounce made her offer, I didn't give a lot of

thought to the potential problems posed by Tony's notoriety for embarking on gargantuan benders. I was too excited at the prospect of working with him. It's not often one is invited to direct a star of his calibre. I mean, I loved the man. Almost everybody did, even those he jettisoned along the road. The main trouble was he didn't love himself, and maybe that's why he never fully comprehended how much his public cared about him. In Australia it went even deeper. There his fans idolised him.

I knew he was on the skids. Everyone in show business knew it. His last few television series and his films had proved dismal flops, but regardless of how close he sailed towards his nemesis, he retained my admiration and that of millions of others who remembered the good times, the times when he was Hhhhhancock, Purveyor of Pleasure to the Great British public and a large part of the English-speaking world.

A number of people warned me that Hancock was a bastard to work with. Some were scathing. 'You're mad,' I was told, 'out of your mind.' 'He's totally uncontrollable.' 'He'll do exactly what he wants to do.' 'He's become a megalomaniac.'

Other comments were more generous: 'He demands the best.' 'He has no time or patience with anyone who doesn't put their absolute all into their work.' I preferred to hear these remarks which reflected my approach to my profession. Rumour had it that Tony was given to tantrums on set. In his book *Tony Hancock*, Philip Oakes wrote that he was 'A star whose unpredictable changes of mood could paralyse a film set.' But I found him completely professional. When he was sober. He craved for perfection but never achieved it after *Hancock's Half-Hour*. He didn't display temperament on set, and I knew when he was unhappy because he'd go to his dressing room and sulk with a large drink until I had time to join him.

Keen as I was to work with him, I felt it prudent to first talk to Tony personally before making a final commitment. I had no intention of waiting until I reached Oz to find out if we were compatible.

At first I chose to think that his personal problems were interfering with his enormous creativity, and I felt that once he got

6

his teeth into something as challenging as a colour series for international distribution, to be shot on 35-millimetre film, he'd forego the booze and scale ever greater comedic heights.

Of course we had disagreements, but we had agreed to disagree on some things. Once when a scene wasn't working after a number of takes, I called a break and went to Tony's dressing room to talk things through. I told him what I thought was wrong. He glared at me. 'What the fuck,' he demanded, 'do you know about comedy?'

When Hancock poses a question like that, there can only be one answer – nothing! He seemed well pleased with the effect his question had on me. After more retakes it still didn't work, and I asked him if he'd do me a favour and at least try it my way. He reluctantly agreed and we had another go. At the end of the take, Tony sporting a large grin, told me, 'You're the first bugger to ever direct me.' I wasn't sure that other directors, particularly the late, great Duncan Wood and Dennis Main Wilson, would have agreed with Tony's assessment, but it still gives me pleasure remembering it. I only wish I'd had a witness.

Tony hit his professional rock bottom in 1967 with a spectacular TV flop by way of *Hancock's*, a series in which he played a nightclub host introducing a string of middle of the road guests in a cheapo production from the UK's ABC Television, who should have known better since a year earlier they had employed Tony to introduce *The Blackpool Show*, which he hated so much that he went AWOL on the last two of eight programmes. Management condemned *Hancock's* for dropping from eight million to 'only' five million viewers.

His talent was, tragically, regrettably, too great for him to handle when mixed with 80° proof. He didn't, couldn't, understand it and when, on the last night of his brief life, he may have tried to analyse it, it destroyed him.

Phyllis gave me his telephone number and suggested a time to ring. A gruff, but unmistakable voice said 'Hello.' My first reaction was to call him Mister Hancock, but I thought better of it and said 'Hello, Tony Hancock, my name's Eddie Joffe.' After a few pleasantries, we got down to business. I asked him how the scripts were shaping up, and he said the first two were excellent.

We arranged to meet at Tony's Kensington flat. It was a miserable, murky London day. I arrived as a pilgrim to Mecca. When the door opened, I was shocked. There stood a very small, very hunched, very haggard, almost caricature version of the Tony Hancock I remembered from the halcyon days of *Hancock's Half-Hour*. I stared long and hard at the sad, rubbery, lived-in face, almost convinced that this was not *the* Tony Hancock, but a much older, gaunt, worn-out clone of the great man.

Nor was I prepared for what was inside, or rather not inside, the living room of the modern luxury flat. It had no furniture. Not even a chair. Nothing. No tables, just carpets, curtains, a few books, a comprehensive collection of empty bottles, mainly vodka, a lot of chipped saucers overflowing with butt ends and ash, and on the mantelpiece a few relics of former triumphs – two SFTA* awards for Light Entertainment Personality of the Year, 1957 and 1959.

There was a bleak loneliness about the place, except for one anomaly in the shape of a gigantic teddy bear that was at least five feet high seated and may well have been another two feet taller if it could stand. Tony had bought the bear in Hong Kong, where he'd been doing cabaret. He claimed that the airline had taken advantage of him by using his name for publicity purposes without payment or even upgrading him to First Class on his flight. He asked them in advance if he could bring a teddy bear aboard. They said, 'Yes of course, Mr Hancock.' To the astonishment and horror of the cabin crew, Tony and a friend lugged this enormous toy on board. There was nowhere to stow it, so it had to have a seat of its own all the way from the Far East to London. Tony chuckled as he recalled that his teddy bear had travelled First Class on BOAC – British Overseas Airways Corporation as it was before the name was changed to British Airways. When he

* SFTA, the Society of Film and Television Arts – now BAFTA, the British Academy of Film and Television Arts.

reached home he found that the bear had actually been made in England. The memory of this discovery sent him into a fit of giggles.

Tony offered me a coffee and shuffled off to make it, returning with a mug of tepid instant. I doubt he'd bothered to bring the kettle back to the boil after his last cup.

We both sat on the floor, he in front of the teddy bear, using its legs as if they were the arms of an armchair, leaning back on its protruding stomach. This provided an indelible memory, but I still wish I'd taken a camera along.

To describe him as uptight would be an understatement. He was like a coiled spring. He didn't remain still for long and spent much of the afternoon pacing to and fro as if he were a caged animal, chainsmoking and irritatingly cutting conversations short every now and then by disappearing for a few minutes to make more ghastly, sweet, black, instant coffee. I took advantage of his absences to skim through the scruffy scripts he'd handed me.

He said he wanted to make a new start in Australia because he was fed up with what he called the dog-eat-dog situation which, he claimed, prevailed throughout British television.

He turned to the subject of TV comedy and how we, or rather he, wanted the series to shape up.

'Where do you think the essence of my work lies?' he asked.

My answer was to frame my head, chin to hair, with flattened hands, indicating a big close-up. He beamed a Cheshire cat grin at me. 'Right,' he purred, 'we'll get on fine. We're in business.' We shook hands. 'With comedy you must be in favour of going in really close. Close-ups,' he continued, 'close-ups of a flicker of an eye are more valuable than the best lines in the show. With some of the *Half-Hours* we moved up from about a hundred and ten shots to about two hundred and seventy-five – really fast cutting. This turned a static situation into something that really moved. I'm particularly concerned about this because many directors I've worked with, particularly recently, have shot from too far away and you can't see a thing. To me this is not television.'

Not everyone would agree with Tony's theory of fast cutting

during slow comedy, a theory he may well have imposed on the shows. Writing in the BFI television quarterly *Contrast*, Derek Hill observed: 'It has taken quite a time for the writers to realise that they, like Hancock, are at their best when next to nothing is going on.' He was referring to the last series Tony did with BBC TV. 'The cuts,' Hill wrote, 'from full-face to profile, the camera movements and the changes of angle usually spring from a cautiousness about being too static, an unnecessary adherence to theory.'

As the afternoon progressed, Tony became more garrulous and more relaxed. At the time, I didn't suspect that he was lacing his awful coffee with another, more volatile, liquid.

Although there was an undertone of a complete lack of confidence about him, we nevertheless warmed to each other and laughed a lot that afternoon, which I felt was a good omen because, in my experience, people who laugh together usually work well together. He showed me his potter's thumb, a thumb which can bend backwards to form a curve for shaping pottery on a wheel. He was very proud of this and demonstrated how he'd used it to bowl googlies, which is a highly desirable skill in the game of cricket. 'Larwood,' he stated, 'would give a lot for a thumb like this.' That remark found its way into one of our scripts.

Michael Wale arrived later in the afternoon. He had been hired by John Collins to write 'additional dialogue'. Neither of us had heard of him before, but his enthusiasm was impressive. Being pressed for time, we concentrated on a broad discussion of the scripts received from Hugh Stuckey, an Australian writer in Melbourne. We were unanimous that a great deal of work was needed on them.

The three of us parted with the feeling that we had established the nucleus of a good working relationship.

Phyllis Rounce was, of course, delighted and not a little relieved that Tony and I had established a rapport. There was one major snag. The Australians wanted the production to start yesterday.

2

'As I was saying before I fell off the stage...'

That first meeting took place on 25 February 1968. A mere ten days later Tony was booked to fly to Oz via India, and the Australians wanted me to accompany him. This was manifestly impossible as my current production commitments could not be completed in under a month. Selfishly, I wanted to fly to Australia via the USA in order to attend the Emmy Awards presentation ceremony staged by the National Academy of Television Arts and Sciences in Washington, DC, because my documentary film *The Price Of A Record*, about the life and death of speed king Donald Campbell, had received a nomination.

Tony had great respect and admiration for John Freeman, who had interviewed him so tellingly in depth on BBC Television's *Face to Face*. Freeman was a shrewd, penetrative interviewer whose technique was closer to psychiatry than journalism. The stark, sterile studio was deliberately designed more as a confessional than a TV setting. It was totally black, and Freeman and his guest – victim may be a better word – were surrounded by black drapes through which the camera lenses poked unobtrusively and concentrated on the subject, never on Freeman, whose remorselessly polite questions were as incisive as a surgeon's scalpel. Freeman was on his best form when interviewing Tony, and fortunately the recording, which has survived, is an object lesson to wannabe interviewers. Tony bared his soul to Freeman. This unlikely pair became close personal friends to the extent that Tony occasionally borrowed the Freeman family flat in Hampstead.

John Freeman had been appointed British High Commissioner to India, and Tony broke his journey to Australia to see him. Freeman refused to discuss that visit with me, but his then wife Catherine told me that John admired Tony enormously. Tony, in turn, often told people that John Freeman should be Prime Minister of Great Britain.

Catherine could not remember much about Tony's sojourn in India except that: 'He wasn't in good form at all. He was drinking and he was absolutely lost with that. He really couldn't cope. He wasn't in good shape. We thought that he was depressed and pretty low.'

In a letter to his mistress written shortly afterwards, Tony reported: 'Saw John Freeman and had lunch and dinner with them.' On another evening Tony dined with a rajah. 'This was dull as hell,' he wrote, 'and until you've heard an Indian band playing Gilbert and Sullivan you haven't lived. Sometimes it is terribly formal over here. After dinner all the ladies are carefully shepherded out to another room while the gentlemen smoke cigars and chat. Very colonial. There is terrible poverty here, though I hear this is not one of the worst areas. I was quite glad to leave. It was rather like being stuck among hundreds of Peter Sellers or being in the middle of Wales with everybody blacked up.'

From India Tony flew to Melbourne to work on the scripts with Hugh Stuckey.

In the previous October (1967), impresario John Collins had imported Tony to Australia to appear at the Dendy Theatre in Brighton, Melbourne. One night Tony fell off the stage. Drunk. The cover story was that someone had laced his tomato juice. The fact was he'd been on a binge with British crooner Matt Monro. On the following Sunday Tony gave a free performance for the audience who'd booed him off. If nothing else immortalised Tony Hancock, it was that Sunday night's opening line: 'As I was saying before I fell off the stage...' The tough Aussie audience melted, forgave him and cheered him to the rafters.

Anxious to keep Tony sober, Collins told Stuckey, who was working for him at the time, 'We've got to keep him busy.' Which is how Hugh entered the frame and began work on a sitcom script with Tony for John Collins.

Essential as it was for Tony's script input, which was basically to personalise the dialogue, Hugh Stuckey's creativity was thwarted in trying to keep him entertained and away from the drink. But how?

'Well, we didn't entirely succeed there,' Hugh admits, 'because I used to spend a lot of time during the day with him, talking about what we were going to do with the TV show.

'I included him a fair bit with my family. I had two daughters and Shirley, my wife, would hand him a small can of beer. She'd ration him. She controlled the grog.'

Nights were a different matter. Alone, without diversions like Stuckey family picnics or watching cricket matches with Hugh, Tony indulged in some serious drinking.

'I was literally his keeper,' Hugh remembers, ' 'cos no one else cared. Collins did nothing really, except complain how was the old bastard going to get off the grog?'

When Tony returned to Australia in 1968, Collins deliberately kept him in Melbourne, well away from the Sydney limelight in case he caused any untoward incidents. Collins knew that regardless of where he was or who he was with, Tony could precipitate 'untoward incidents' at the drop of an ice cube into a Bloody Mary. Collins told ATN-7 that Hancock was 'in great shape, he just doesn't want to be disturbed, he's working with Stuckey on the script and until the scripts are right, he doesn't want to talk to or see anybody.' And ATN-7 bought that. For a while.

Hugh again looked after Tony with exactly the same measure of success he'd had on the earlier visit: 'He was in a motel here for a long time and he used to get absolutely smashed out of his mind, and I'd go round in the mornings, and in one case I found that he'd actually been on the phone all night. As soon as I walked in the door the manager came running up and said: "Excuse me, Mr Stuckey, can I see you for a minute? Mr Hancock was on the phone to England for something like six hours." He'd gone to sleep, talking to his mother on the phone in England, and the motel were panic-stricken that he wouldn't be able to pay the bill.'

'Collins was under real pressure to present Hancock to the network,' Stuckey recalls, 'and he didn't know what to do to get him off the grog.' Collins informed Stuckey he had rummaged through Tony's bags when Tony was unconscious and found a bank statement. The balance was only a few hundred dollars. 'The best thing to do,' Collins confided to Hugh, 'is to let him drink it as quickly as possible, then he'll have to work.' When Collins again checked through Tony's luggage, he found that the bank account had been exhausted and closed. Only he'd overlooked another bank account reflecting a very healthy balance amounting to tens of thousands of dollars from Tony's previous Australian tour!

The series was to be produced in Sydney, and ATN-7 wanted him there to meet him and get him and the writers on the case the minute Mike Wale touched down. When the time came for Tony to leave Melbourne he had a panic attack and put his arms round Shirley Stuckey. 'He was crying,' Hugh told me, 'he said, "Please don't make me go. Please stop them. Please stop them." Yeah, he knew what he was in for...'

Hugh Stuckey accompanied him on that early morning flight, during which Tony polished off most of the beer on board.

3

'He's still got that sparkle'

My decision to fly via the USA proved to be a bad one. My arrival in New York coincided with the assassination of Martin Luther King. I changed aircraft to get to Washington, and as the almost empty plane circled the airport, the fires lit by rampaging protestors, incensed at the outrage of King's death, could clearly be seen below. It was worse on the ground. The reek of smoke was oppressive. Hundreds of people queued at the airport ticket desks, clamouring for seats on any available aircraft going anywhere else. In the city itself, automobiles sped through the almost deserted streets. I saw excitable passengers hurl bottles, bricks and other missiles at shop windows, stationary cars and any passerby foolish enough to be out of doors. Washington DC, the capital of the United States of America and indeed, most of the free world, was under siege. It was a city peopled by rioters and uniformed, armed militia. Helicopters buzzed about at low level like angry hornets. So serious was the situation that martial law was declared and a curfew imposed from 5.30 p.m., one hour before the Awards Ceremony was due to begin.

As soon as I heard this on a newscast, I telephoned the Mayflower Hotel, where the awards ceremony was to be held, to talk to the organiser, Mr de Santis. The chaos was worse than that at the airport and he couldn't be located, but the Emmy PR man advised me that the event was cancelled and he'd call me back to tell me if my programme had won. When he did call, he was very complimentary about *The Price Of A Record*. It would have won, he said, if it hadn't been for *The Anderson Platoon*. The good news was that my film would receive a plaque. I said I'd collect it.

I had no choice but to walk the four blocks from my hotel to the Mayflower. On my way out, an elderly woman from the National League of Pinwomen heard the porter giving me directions to the Mayflower where she too was heading, and I couldn't refuse her request to walk her there. Due to her age it took a lot longer than the porter's estimated ten minutes for us to reach the Mayflower. Pinwomen? An association of women who work for pin money. Only in America!

On reaching the Mayflower I asked the front desk for the Emmy office, only to have a telephone thrust at me. It was the executive director of the Swedish TV Service. No, I didn't know anything about the ceremony except that it was cancelled. 'Sorry, I can't help,' I said. 'I'm trying to get some myself!' 'You'll never work in Sweden again,' Tony observed when he heard the story.

Eventually I got to speak to the PR man on the internal telephone, who told me that Mr de Santis had left for New York and hadn't said where the plaque would be. Just then a loud-speaker announced that the curfew had been brought forward to 4.30 p.m. I glanced at my watch. It was 4.25. All I could do was scurry back to my hotel.

En route, I watched an army jeep chasing a car bearing the words 'Soul Brother' and 'Soul Sister' painted crudely on its sides. Seconds later a bunch of armed soldiers headed straight at me. It was well past the curfew deadline and I was flouting the law. I remembered I had no ID on me, having left my passport at my hotel. My heart was in my mouth as I conjured up a movie image of the interior of an American jail cell crammed with murderers, rapists, junkies and me.

This time luck was on my side and the GIs ignored me completely as I scuttled past them. I dismissed the thought that they might have been screen extras hired to publicise *The Anderson Platoon*.

Back at my hotel I headed straight for the bar. It was closed. Most of the staff had gone home early to beat the curfew. Fortunately, I'd bought some miniatures on the plane which washed down the only food available in the hotel that night, which happened to be chicken à la king.

After innumerable telephone calls I was eventually connected to the awards organiser at his home in New York. He apologised for the cancellation and assured me that I would have enjoyed the ceremony which was sure to have been 'A very dignified affair – complete with the band of the US Marine Corps.'

Tony was amused at the picture I later painted for him of the events. He loved the idea of a League of Pinwomen and relished the concept of dignity in the presence of the US Marine Corps Band. He said he could imagine it all happening to the accompaniment of the Marine March – 'From the Halls of Montezuma...'

What with my diversion to Washington and my planned stop over in San Francisco to see my brother, I was two days behind schedule. On my way to National Airport I collected the plaque, which the organiser had left with his sister who lived in Washington. The memento, presented to Emmy Award finalists, was a certificate laminated onto a plywood backing. This *objet d'art* shattered my dream of arriving in Sydney clutching a gleaming, gold-plated winner's statuette of a winged angel holding aloft the world. I had hoped that the trophy might somehow excuse my late arrival. An award resembling a table mat was hardly an adequate substitute, so I kept it well concealed and only showed it to Tony. Since I was personally footing the bill for the detour, it proved to be the most expensive table mat I ever owned.

The aircraft landed at a misty Sydney Airport on 9 April 1968. I was welcomed by Geoff Healy, an ATN-7 executive, and John Collins. Healy was a hail-fellow-well-met sort of guy with whom I immediately felt at ease. As far as I knew, Collins was the series producer and he almost precisely matched my mental picture of him – a short, aggressive, wheeler-dealer. Nobody, it seemed, liked Collins, and he and Tony, I soon discovered, were at daggers drawn.

The reason for this antagonism was spawned in Melbourne the previous October, when Hugh began writing the sitcom we were about to work on. When he'd completed the first script Hugh showed it to Collins, who read it. When he'd finished, he said,

17

'It's a load of shit.' And he threw it from one end of the office to the other.

'I immediately got in the car,' Hugh told me, 'and drove to the Savoy Hotel in Brighton where Tony was staying, and showed it to him. He read it and chuckled and when he'd finished, he didn't say anything. He picked up the phone and he rang Collins – I'd told him what Collins had done to me – and Tony said Collins was not to have anything further to do with the scripts. He was not to talk to the writer. He wasn't to speak to anybody about the scripts.'

Collins took me straight to the writers' Sydney hotel for a script conference. It was my first meeting with Hugh Stuckey, an experienced writer well known in Australia for his comedy. I had read several of Hugh's draft scripts on the flight, and although a lot of rewriting was still needed, he had turned out some first-class material. It was encouraging to find that he and Mike Wale had jelled, despite the fact that Hugh Stuckey had no idea that there was to be another writer on the series until he reached Sydney with Tony and was presented with Wale as a *fait accompli*. It developed into one of those fortunate show-business writing collaborations. Hugh was great on situations and Mike had a knack of capturing the Hancockian turn of phrase.

Granted, the scripts weren't up to Galton and Simpson quality. Yet. But they showed great promise, and the symbiosis between the writers was sparking off in all the right directions, then having quickly grasped one of the secrets of writing for Hancock, which was to listen to his anecdotes and utilise them as the basis for scripts and dialogue whenever possible.

Almost as importantly, we all seemed to like each other.

Collins interrupted our creative flow by nagging about how much we had to do that day, such as collecting Tony, going to the studios to meet the ATN people and viewing audition tapes. The script meeting was therefore very short and Collins collected Tony at the Georgian House Hotel. Tony had been into some hard drinking and was not in the best of moods, but my arrival – the mere presence of someone he knew was on his side – cheered him up. But not for long.

The atmosphere between Hancock and Collins was electric and simply awful. The bad vibes between them were tangible, and they weren't even talking to one another. Tony hated Collins with one of those tremendous hates that seemed to be one of the prerequisites of Tony's life. As he saw it, Collins was a conman who had brought him to Australia under false pretenses. Collins therefore became the hook on which Tony hung the blame for the misery in which he was currently wallowing. Tony was in love. Tony missed his woman. Tony was homesick. Tony missed his mother. Tony was unhappy. Tony was worried. Tony's divorce action was hotting up. Tony was lonely. Tony was drinking. Tony was in danger of being sued by the Delfont/Grade Organisation. Tony was bored. All Collins' fault, of course.

In the month he was in Melbourne Tony enriched the telephone company by $1,800 Australian – over £800 sterling – a phenomenal sum in those days. His calls were all to England, to his mistress, his solicitors and his mother. Collins refused to foot the phone bill.

On the drive to ATN-7's Epping studios on the outskirts of Sydney, they made no effort to disguise their antagonism towards each other in my presence, and their remarks were all addressed to and through me.

It was a relief to leave them to it when we reached the ATN-7 studios, where Geoff Healy gave me a whistlestop tour. The station itself was far larger and better equipped than I had imagined.

The studio we were to work in was big: 90 feet by 70, resplendent with shiny, new Arriflex Electronic Camera (E-CAM) equipment standing by to take Tony to the top.

Since ATN-7 wanted to start shooting as soon as I arrived, set construction for the first programme was already well in hand. I understood their decision to press on with things in my absence, but I'd never before encountered a series where the art department was unable to obtain directorial input. I therefore asked for, and got, some essential modifications to the set for first studio filming, due in ten days' time.

It wasn't an ideal way to start a series, but sets and props weren't a priority with me because the success of the series would hinge on the quality of Tony's performance, regardless of how splendid or indifferent the sets happened to be.

The room in which we viewed the auditions was crowded. In a letter home dated Good Friday 1968, I wrote: 'He's still got that sparkle and although it was done on a gash tape which had been shot in a hurry without any planning, it was impressive.'

Tony had himself read his lines to the hopefuls who wanted to work with him, and the audition tapes boosted my enthusiasm for the project. Tony was absolutely marvellous. He had obviously studied the scripts thoroughly, and his lines took on a new dimension when he delivered them. They jumped from the cold print on the page and became, well, vintage Hancock. My judgments on the auditioning artistes' capabilities were easily gauged. Those who had interacted best with Tony were contracted.

My Good Friday letter home continued: 'To crown the viewing session, Collins fell asleep which infuriated Tony who has been brooding about this ever since.'

This provided the tinder which sparked the final conflagration between them. Tony paid scant attention to the playback and sat glowering at the gently snoring Collins, whose behaviour Tony regarded as the supreme insult. Tony was not one to mince words with people he regarded as fools. He would not tolerate any kind of inefficiency or stupidity, and in his view Collins was guilty of both these cardinal sins. On the way home the feud erupted into a saloon bar slanging match. Collins told me later that he'd been up since 5 a.m. to get to the airport to meet me after having had a very late night, and that he was absolutely exhausted. So was I, jetlagged out of my mind, but I managed to keep going on an overdose of adrenalin.

Tony was not prepared to accept Collins' 'excuse' and he took to telephoning me every few hours – not only because he was lonely, but because he wanted to know how long it would be before we could 'get Collins off the show'. My attempts to placate Tony were a waste of breath.

One of the major irritants, I later discovered, was that Tony was under contract to a company called Willard King which, as far as I knew, belonged to Collins, so in effect Tony was under contract to

20

Collins personally – and not to ATN-7. Tony saw Collins as the guy with total control over his strings and, to put it mildly, Tony was not a happy puppet. ATN-7 were well aware of the friction between them and, unbeknown to me or Tony, the station management were negotiating with Collins to buy Tony's contract from him.

A project as ambitious as the one we were about to embark upon called for months of careful pre-planning – a far cry from the paltry ten days I had in which to try to finalise details for the first half-dozen scheduled shows. I pointed out to the ATN-7 management that the impossible could be done immediately, but miracles would take a little longer, and unless more time was scheduled for pre-production planning, they were not to expect too much from the first show. I made it clear to them that the first programme had to be regarded as a 'pilot', which is TV jargon for a try-out, and meant that if it wasn't up to standard in any area, it would have to be re-shot in its entirety.

During meetings, no one referred to John Collins, who fidgeted in his chair contributing zilch to the discussion and looking extremely bored with the proceedings. His attitude and the way he lorded it over some people led me to assume that he was my producer. No one had told me otherwise and, observing his behaviour, another contributing factor in Tony's intense dislike of Collins became clear – he was utterly uninterested in the production. Nevertheless, he too nodded agreement to my insistence that the first programme be considered a pilot.

The management did not exactly perform a jig of joy about this prospect, but they realised that we were, after all, about to work on revolutionary new equipment with technicians who were not familiar with it, and they, the cast, and the rest of the creative people had to be forged into a team. Management were naturally anxious to get Tony on the studio floor. They wanted quick results. They wanted to see what they were getting for their money. They wanted something to show the board of directors, and they insisted I press on regardless of my misgivings about pushing Tony, and everyone else, in at the deep end so quickly.

My recommendations were accepted by ATN-7's management

21

for the wrong reasons. I suspect they thought I was worrying unnecessarily and that, somehow, it would be all right on the night.

Channel 7 had assembled some first-class people. My production assistant, Clare Richardson, had worked for the BBC in London and for the Australian Broadcasting Company in Sydney. She was a tactful, talented, loyal, charming, intelligent young woman who, 30 years on, insists she was: 'A frivolous and light-hearted person who wasn't terribly involved and had other agendas going on.' Her perspicacious, poignant, contemporary letters written to her parents in London belie her preferred description.

On 1 April 1968, a mere week before I reached Sydney, Clare had written: 'The lovely Channel 7 job has fallen through. I shouldn't really have told you about it so enthusiastically because it was on the cards that it would fold – though one never actually thinks these things will. As you know the series relies on Tony Hancock, who is a *passé* drunkard, trying to re-establish himself in Australia.'

She went on to mention Hancock's failures, then added: 'In any case, for the lack of a team, scripts, and Hancock himself, the series doesn't look as if it'll be off the ground for months.' This was the only inaccurate prediction she made, and two weeks later we started rehearsals.

The writers had to be left to themselves. Tony's creative input was only needed for a few hours now and again. Their tight deadlines did not allow Hugh and Mike time to devote to Tony's insatiable need for a shoulder to lean on. Left to his own devices, Tony could be relied upon to get truly well oiled. Not that it took a great quantity of alcohol for him to do that, because, not to put too fine a point on it, his biological system was about 90 proof and all he needed were a couple of tots to top him up.

My other assistant, Dusty Nelson, was a young man who had worked with Tony as his floor manager in London. We both liked Dusty, and it was he who filled me in on certain details of the John Collins saga. Dusty knew his way around the studios and his duties were to liaise between ATN-7's numerous service and technical departments, but regrettably, his main contribution to the series was one which nobody could have forecast...

The rest of the crew were the best the Australians had. They were mostly young. All were keen. And what they lacked in experience was compensated for by their enthusiasm. They were raring to get cracking on what everyone saw as a breakthrough in Australian television terms – the first ever series to be shot on 35mm colour film employing the latest state-of-the-art equipment, aimed at the international market, and featuring one of the best-known, best-loved comedians in the English-speaking world outside the USA. They were all determined to give their all. And more.

4

''Ancock's 'ere! In person!'

Wednesday 10 April 1968, my second day in Australia, was spent on auditions for a few cameo roles, under the guidance of one Franz Conde of the ATN-7 Talent Department. Franz, a small Austrian, who had composed a number of internationally popular songs, talked like Cuddles Szakall, and knew everybody who was anybody in Australian show business and most of those of any importance who weren't.

'In Vienna,' he'd boast, 'I vos a dachshund. Here, I'm a Great Dane.' The ATN-7 schedule had forced him to contract key performers in my absence for fear of losing them and, with one exception, he'd done a very good job.

Franz and I finalised the cast for the first programme to be recorded.

I had been installed in an office commensurate with the importance ATN-7 attached to the series. It happened to be the infrequently used chairman's suite, a splendidly furnished, spacious office next to that of the Managing Director. If I needed or wanted anything, I had only to say so and no matter what the request, it was fulfilled almost immediately.

I now had to apply myself to the creative planning of artistes' and camera moves, a job I preferred to do in peace and quiet at my hotel, where there were no interruptions. This also bought me a few extra working hours each day by saving travel time to the studios and back.

Invariably, a person of Tony's calibre visiting Australia to star in a high-profile, prestigious television series would have generated publicity junkets from the ATN-7 press office, who would have ensured that he attended public and private functions to be entertained and lionised by Sydney celebrities and socialites. He would have given press conferences and 'exclusive' interviews and made guest appearances on some of the ATN-7 talk shows which featured interesting, newsworthy people. In the normal course of events, the ATN-7 press office would have built up the publicity panoply to help the series attract advance interest in an eagerly awaited series.

But ATN-7 was fidgety. When Tony first arrived in Australia, there'd been a press conference at which he was asked the name of the series. He said 'Marie'. At least that's what the Press heard. There was a Mary in his life – his London housekeeper – whose name he sometimes called out when he was in his cups. Someone suggested that 'Marie' was Tony's *Citizen Kane* Rosebud, but he may simply have been in an alcoholic haze and, forgetting where he was, wanted Mary to fetch something he needed and slurred her name. Well, maybe that is a bit cynical and the other, most likely assumption is that Tony was just being wicked and taking the piss out of the Press. Whatever the reason, *'Marie'* was the name the media latched on to and which stuck to the series.

Despite Collins' precautions, stories of Tony's prodigious Melbourne drinking sprees had filtered back to ATN-7 in Sydney, 600 miles away. So when he reached Sydney ATN-7 opted to keep him under wraps. They were reluctant to allow him or the production any publicity because they feared the possibility of embarrassing scenes. The management were having doubts about the potential strength or weakness of the series, and after the *'Marie'* experience they felt that the lower they kept the Hancock profile the better. They were working on the least said, soonest mended theory.

Clare wrote home: 'My job was to keep wardrobe, make-up, designers, props, set dressers etc, fully informed and have the script, which was changed and hacked to bits, retyped. No typists could be found, so I had to do the job myself, and was putting in a 10 or so hour day, every day.'

Things were hotting up and I was spending 15 hours a day not so much trying to keep ahead of the game, but catching it up. The writers continued to beaver away.

With all our hectic activity our star was being neglected, and his liquid intake increased in direct proportion to his boredom.

It wasn't that he wanted to be fêted, and although he was very entertaining when interviewed he had the shadow of a libel suit looming large, triggering anxiety about what journalists might write about or attribute to him. Tony needed someone to talk to whenever the urge came upon him. It was obviously impossible for him to continuously phone England for his human contact. The staff at his hotel were remarkably loyal to him. He would abuse them, swear at them, call them for firewater or sandwiches at all hours of the day or night, and they tolerated his outrageous behaviour with good-natured humour and never uttered a word against him. Possibly they all realised that he was going through a very rough time in a strange country without any close friends.

I wanted to spend as much time as I could with Tony to get to know him better. I wanted to get as close to the real Hancock as he would allow, to find out, if that was possible, what made him tick. Therefore, my time was almost totally monopolised by Tony Hancock both as a programme and as a person.

Forward planning is essential, and only the director can produce camera scripts, which are required at least four weeks in advance of studio production. The director must chair meetings with members of all service departments to discuss details of the hundred and one requirements for each and every programme. Rehearsals cannot be held without the director present at every rehearsal, every day. That's four days a week. Studio filming took two days a week, which left one day for viewing the rushes, meetings, forward planning and preparing camera scripts. Thirteen shows were scheduled over the next 13 weeks, so time was not on my side.

One night after working late at the studios, I dropped in to see Tony on my way home. When I asked the receptionist how he was, she smiled and shook her head as usual. His door was unlocked and his room was in its normal chaotic mess. Tony was fast asleep, stark naked, on the bed, but the light from the opening door woke him. He ordered coffee and sandwiches for us, and when the maid knocked he called out to her to enter. She couldn't have been more than 17 and Tony didn't have a stitch on, but the young woman didn't bat an eyelid at what was obviously not her first eyeful of a nude Tony Hancock.

Everyone who knew Tony was aware of his inherent shyness and his reluctance to get to know strangers, preferring to contemplate the bottom of a glass, only putting it down long enough to indulge in his other horrific habit of picking up the telephone and calling whoever he felt like talking to at any time of the day or night.

He telephoned the writers and me incessantly. John Collins was the dominant topic and the conversations, mainly venomous monologues about Collins, could last up to an hour. I several times told him I was trying to get the show on the road and hung up, only to have him call back five minutes later, when he would again plough the identical furrow, having probably forgotten his earlier 'chat' and the ones before that.

On the night before Good Friday Tony phoned me so often that I was forced to leave the phone off its hook. Next morning, a public holiday, I was working on camera scripts and being interrupted by Tony every 20 minutes or so. I had visions of this continuing the entire weekend, but it was impractical to have the phone disconnected all the time as I needed contact with Hugh and Mike. In desperation I rang Collins and told him he had to find a way to get Tony off my back that weekend, because it was essential for me to complete my planning in order to pass full technical requirements to the crew on Easter Monday.

'Right,' said Collins, 'I'll send someone to see you. Have a chat with him and tell him what you want done.'

A few hours later, a man called Durham showed up saying he'd been sent by John Collins to 'look after Tony Hancock'. I pondered on how to tell Tony that this guy was to be his minder and decided to introduce Durham as a friend, then withdraw and leave the two of them together. I rang Tony and told him we were on our way to see him.

27

'Come right round,' he said happily, 'have lunch here.'

By the time we reached his hotel, Tony had finished his first course. He informed us he'd eaten a bad oyster so he ordered a double brandy to 'settle his stomach'. When the bill arrived Tony's lunchtime score was a bottle of wine, a large brandy and three liqueurs.

He looked pretty bloody, so we took him to a chemist where he requested a concoction normally only available on prescription. The pharmacist recognised him and, knowing it would be consumed there and then, he gave Tony what he wanted. Tony knocked it back and immediately demanded another, but the chemist refused on the grounds that it would kill him. Tony was adamant. I took the chemist aside and asked him for a liquid placebo and told Tony it was another dose of his prescription which he could take later. Having thus pacified him we left, with the pharmacist sighing and shaking his head.

I felt the best thing for Tony would be some fresh air. Very reluctantly he agreed. He didn't much go for the outdoor life and was astonished at the way Australians 'keep bounding and leaping and jumping about all over the place' – another line that found its way into a script.

There was no way I would allow Tony to return to his hotel as he requested. I was sure he'd drink himself into oblivion if he did, so I suggested we visit the Royal Easter Show at the Sydney Showground.

When we arrived there, Tony's pleasant hooch-induced euphoria had worn off and he clicked into recalcitrant mode. He'd take a few Napoleonic paces forward, stop with his hands behind his back, frown at the world and root himself into the ground, mumbling, grumbling.

I realised too late that it was a blunder taking him to so crowded a place where people gathered around him in a friendly way, politely requesting autographs and mouthing platitudes like: 'I'm a great fan of yours.' 'We always watch your shows.' 'When are we going to see you on television again?' or simply 'Hello *Mr* Hancock.'

Everyone recognised him and most claimed fan status. Tony glared or grinned, as the mood took him.

To shelter him from the masses, we went into a large hall. Inside, Tony became riveted by the antics of a woman selling perfume at one of the stalls. She was working with a microphone, striving to imitate a Cockney market stallholder in a broad, almost incomprehensible Australian accent. She soon spotted Tony staring at her, fascinated. For her this was a once in a lifetime business opportunity, and she started shouting, ''Ullo Mr 'Ancock. Come over 'ere. Folks, Mr Tony 'Ancock's 'ere! In person!' She quickly attracted dozens of people to her previously neglected stall. When she leaned across and squirted some ghastly cheap scent all over him with the admonition: 'Try some o' that, love – you'll be an 'it with all the ladies,' I thought Tony was going to have a fit of embarrassment. Before anything ugly took place I tried to steer him away, but he barked at me, 'Don't you paw me...' He hated physical contact.

Nevertheless our new 'friend' Durham came to the rescue and helped me bundle Tony outside to a less crowded section of the fairground. We paused for breath near one of those shadowgraph tents where they cut your silhouetted profile from black paper. I asked Tony to pose for a personal souvenir for me. Leaving him in Durham's care, I went for a pee and returned to find Tony holding the hand of a small girl aged about eight, who was having her silhouette done. This child had a very beautiful, innocent face and long, plaited golden hair. For me this was a totally unexpected facet of Tony's character. I hadn't imagined him liking kids.

He may well have sat there the whole afternoon if the girl's parents hadn't taken her away when the silhouette was completed. Tony reluctantly waved goodbye to the family and lumbered towards a tent marked 'Bar', where he was greatly annoyed, indeed disgusted, to find that the only drinks on sale were soft.

'Come on, Don,' he said, 'time to get out of here.' Tony had decided that Durham bore a resemblance to the legendary Don Bradman. Durham was also a cricket fanatic, hardly surprising for an Australian.

Cricket was high on the list of Tony's favourite topics. He

could have bored for England on the subject, which he would natter on about to anyone who cared to listen, and 'Don' was being paid to listen. Tony was an extremely keen follower of the game. He'd been known to stay in bed all day to listen to radio commentaries. He had his mother mail him newspaper cuttings about matches whenever he was away from England. Once during a stage engagement at the Adelphi Theatre in London, he'd conned a doctor into giving him a sick note to allow him time off from his show to attend a Test Match at Lord's, the home of world cricket. Test matches last five days...

In Melbourne Hugh Stuckey took some cricketing friends, who happened to be famous Test Match players, to see Tony's show, after which Tony invited them to his dressing room.

Hugh remembers: 'Tony sat there with his grotty old short dressing gown over his underpants, and they talked cricket for about two hours while I entertained the wives in a corner. When they eventually went home, Hancock just sat there with this starry-eyed look on his face and he said, "They won't believe it, you know, they won't believe it when I get back home and say I had Norm O'Neill and Len Maddocks all to myself for two hours." Norm and Len will say, no one will believe we had Tony Hancock all to ourselves for two hours.'

'Don' dropped me off, and he and Tony drove away cheerfully chatting cricket. I went back to my work feeling relaxed in the knowledge that Tony had found a soul mate. Best of all, 'Don' would release Dusty for production work. Wrong!

Early next morning the phone shrilled. It was Tony, and he was irate.

'This Don Bradman chap's here,' he snapped, 'has he been put in as a watchdog?'

'He's there to drive you around wherever you want to go,' I answered.

'I want you to get rid of him,' Tony demanded.

'You do need a driver,' I countered.

'Not this one,' he grouched.

Maybe they'd run out of cricket conversation, or maybe 'Don' wasn't up to a sober Tony's intellectual requirements or whatever.

30

I never did find out, but it didn't matter because Tony had developed a dislike to him, and that was it!

My need to concentrate on pre-production precluded the social contact we both wanted, and I told Tony so for the umpteenth time.

'Hang on to him for a few days,' I suggested, 'see how you get along.'

Tony grunted, rang off and didn't phone again that day, allowing me to almost complete what I'd set out to do, so 'Don' didn't do a bad job after all.

I worked most of Saturday except for an hour I took off to visit the Wayside Chapel in nearby King's Cross, to check if John Collins was telling the truth when he'd mentioned he was getting married that day. He was and he did. I congratulated him and his bride, threw a bit of confetti and returned to work.

5

'Let's get rid of this boy'

Apart from Tony's alcohol addiction, his other compulsion – to have someone to hate – wasn't limited to people he felt may have harmed him in some way. I could understand his feelings about Collins, but after Collins disappeared he vented his spleen on the minions.

When a young, inexperienced floor manager replaced the original floor manager, he was overawed by Tony and treated him like a demigod. I never fathomed why he sparked off such antagonism in Tony, who took an instant and intense dislike to him and kept saying, 'Let's get rid of this boy.' We were unable to do so as no one else was available, and the unfortunate guy had a very miserable time of it in the studio.

Another example of this mean streak emerged after a phone call I received from a young man who claimed he was Tony's cousin from New Zealand, in Sydney on holiday. He wanted to know how to contact Tony. We were used to fending off phone calls from oddballs wanting photographs or autographs or for Tony to make an appearance at some local event, and they weren't above subterfuge to achieve their aims. None had thus far penetrated the Hancock Curtain, so I quizzed the caller and asked if Tony would know him and he said, 'No, but Aunt Lil – Mrs Sennett – said to ring him.' This sounded plausible enough to me, since I doubted if many people knew Tony's mother's full name. After warning the caller of my doubts that Tony would give him much time, I invited him along to the studio. When he turned up I told Tony about him.

'He's no relative of mine,' Tony stated. I suggested that a few minutes with him wouldn't hurt, and even if he weren't really his cousin, his enterprise at least warranted an hello. 'No,' Tony insisted, 'I don't want to see him.' And he didn't. The lad was very disappointed, but accepted it gracefully.

Tony refused to allow 'Don Bradman' to pick him up for work on the Easter Monday read-through and had, in effect, fired him. It's possible that 'Don' may have mentioned Collins' name to Tony who, by then, was calling Collins a cunt to his face.

Collins wasn't available for discussion. He'd gone on his honeymoon without telling me, or anyone else for that matter, of his plans one way or another – so I told Geoff Healy what had happened over the weekend with 'Don Bradman'.

Healy informed me that a deal had been concluded with Collins, whose contract with Tony had been bought out and Collins no longer had anything to do with the production. Healy felt that since the main obstacle to Hancock's peace of mind had now been removed, he hoped this would enable the production to progress more smoothly.

Although I had not been privy to the negotiations, I was relieved that Collins was no longer in the picture so to speak, but I was totally unprepared for Healy's next statement. He casually mentioned that I was now the producer. While this was sinking in, he threw me a second body punch by asking who I would like to have direct the series!

There is a thin dividing line between the duties of a producer and those of a director. As it happens, the trend for these two jobs to be carried out by the same person is on the increase, and some producers direct and many directors produce. In broad terms, when the jobs are separated and two people are involved, the producer is generally an administrator or responsible in the first place for raising money or for eliciting interest from broadcasters or other production companies to commission a series based on the producer's concept, or all these things. The producer will generally choose a director to work on the creative side. In a number of cases, a producer will engage a director in the early stages of pre-production. Conversely, a director may take a project to a producer to help develop and finance the 'property'.

My preference is to direct rather than produce, since I find directing more satisfying creatively than the burden of overseeing the finances and the minutiae of administration. I was not prepared to forego the pleasure of directing the show, and I told Healy that a change was out of the question at that late stage and in any case Tony would not accept anyone else as his director. My suggestion was that ATN-7 should instead find another producer to look after the admin for me. The company rejected this as it was more cost-effective for them to deploy a staff director to the Hancock series than to employ a freelance producer. Although I had in fact been carrying out a producer's duties because of Collins' lack of interest, henceforth I was officially producer *and* director.

As full responsibility for the production now devolved on me, I felt my fee had to be renegotiated as I was not prepared to accept the additional responsibility of being producer, director, script editor and fall guy all for the price of a director. No way.

This precipitated a chain of events which I could ill afford to waste time on so close to the first studio production day. In those pre-fax, pre-internet days of yore, letters, telephone calls, cablegrams and telexes galore began flowing between Jack Neary's Sydney office and Hugh Alexander at International Artistes in London, and from thence to ATN-7 and to Neary and back again... In order to allow me to concentrate on my series, I had to distance myself from the negotiations since shooting was a mere four days away.

6

'He thought he fell in love all the time'

People often ask why Tony chose to make an Australian series. The answer is quite simple. Nobody in the UK wanted to work with him. One day he would expose his soul in a flood of alcohol-induced emotion, the next he'd disappear into his private clam shell, broody, sullen, aloof and withdrawn, as difficult to approach as an electrified fence.

Tony's personal Holy Grail was to achieve recognition in the USA. This was long before Benny Hill became a cult attraction there. In the Sixties it was doubtful that the Americans liked, appreciated, or even cared about English comedy because their style and tastes differed enormously from ours. Few Americans, apart from television programme buyers, had ever seen any British comedy, and those who did claimed they needed subtitles to understand them. And if there's anything that the Great American Television Public abhors, it's subtitles. Benny's shows went down so well across the Atlantic in the Eighties because the Yanks didn't need subtitles to understand his raunchy sketches. The same applied to *Monty Python* – another very visual show consisting of short, sharp sketches, loads of clever animations, oodles of special effects and packed with sight gags – a far cry from the 'situation comedy' genre invented in the Fifties by Ray Galton and Alan Simpson for Tony Hancock's radio shows, which transferred seamlessly to television and considerable public acclaim.

In the 1950s and '60s most American TV comics seemed to be

of the stand-up Vaudeville/Bob Hope type. Bob Hope admits to 140 jokes per half-hour show, which is one every 12.85 seconds... Their television comedies were almost all fast-movin', fast-talkin' productions, such as *I Love Lucy*, *The Dick Van Dyke Show* and *The Phil Silvers Show (Sergeant Bilko)*. The USA had nothing remotely as subtle as *Hancock's Half-Hour*, which was totally unique.

Hancock was himself unique in that his work was universally admired by everyone, from lowbrow to eggheads, from paupers to millionaires. Right across the social spectrum people were able to identify with this bumbling bombast at odds with the world about him. At his peak he could have read the telephone directory, merely raised an eyebrow, or hinted at a smile or a disapproving frown to send his regular audience of about 13 million Brits into paroxysms of delight.

For Tony, the beginning of the end started in the late Fifties when, bored with his East Cheam image, he decided he had to make his mark in motion pictures. These, surely, he reckoned, would give him his yearned-for *entrée* to the United States.

Ray Galton confirmed this: 'In his own mind Tony had to prove he was an international star, and the only way to be an international star in this world, dominated by the Americans, is to appeal to the Americans and be taken up and make Hollywood films.'

Hancock's first movie, *The Rebel*, written by Galton and Simpson, was far from a box-office smash. It acquired a few plaudits from British critics, but the Americans savaged it. This rankled Tony until he died.

By 1960, Tony had ditched Sid James and most of the *Hancock's Half-Hour* repertory players.

Galton and Simpson started work on a second screenplay for Tony. About halfway through, after three months' unpaid labour, Tony rejected their script. They suggested a new theme, which he accepted then again rejected another three months later.

Associated London Scripts – ALS – was a creative company set up by Galton, Simpson, Eric Sykes and Spike Milligan. It was administered by Beryl Vertue, and she was Tony's agent. Tony called a meeting with 'the boys' as he generally referred to them – a patronising sobriquet they greatly resented. Beryl Vertue and Tony's brother Roger were also summoned. 'The week leading up to this meeting was really quite tense,' Beryl Vertue recalls. 'Ray and Alan were writing a film script for him, and he didn't seem to like it quite, and it got to the point where he wasn't exactly talking to them directly. It wasn't as though they had a row or anything. He used to say his thoughts through me to them and then they would say their thoughts through me to him! It was extremely uneasy and very unusual, because you're talking about three people who not only worked together – they kind of fitted like a glove really. When Tony spoke ordinarily you almost thought he was speaking their dialogue. It had grown into that kind of absolutely intuitive teaming of talent.'

The fateful meeting took place on a Sunday afternoon at the White House, itself a weird establishment at the time – a sort of half-hotel, half-apartment building just off Euston Road, where Tony had a dingy flat, all cream and brown and dreary.

Beryl said: 'We thought we had gone to sort out this film script – how to get the story right and really discuss what it was Tony didn't like about it. Within minutes he said he didn't want Ray and Alan to write for him any more.'

He then fired Beryl in a simple, matter-of-fact way: 'I think you shouldn't be my agent any more because I'm going to make this change and you're so involved with Alan and Ray,' he told her, 'Roger can do it.'

'We were so stunned by it that actually nobody said anything,' Beryl remembered, 'I mean, nobody had a row and nobody shouted.'

Beryl, Alan and Ray left and went downstairs to the swimming pool: 'It had a kind of decaying grandeur down there. And they had little tables and chairs, and Alan and Ray and I sat there and had a cup of tea, sitting round this pool trying to take it in, and I was trying hard, very hard, not to cry – except I think I did, but not out loud – my eyes were all swimming because it was like somebody died really.'

For Beryl it wasn't just the end of a business arrangement, and she didn't think in terms of losing a famous client, more that a friend had cut her dead.

'I felt really, really sad because it had been a gradual shedding almost, on his part, of the people that were important in his working life because his working life had also become part of his personal life.'

'In many respects he was quite callous,' Alan Simpson told me. 'He did it very cold-bloodedly.'

Tony turned to Philip Oakes to collaborate with him on his new film project. They had first met when Oakes interviewed Tony for a literary magazine. They happened to be neighbours and became firm friends years before starting work on *The Punch and Judy Man*. The story of the binges during that association is graphically sketched in Oakes' book *Tony Hancock*.

'You could see the whole system just being completely wrecked by the lethal intake the whole time. It was extraordinary,' Oakes told me, 'I've never seen such punishing drinking in my life. It was quite awful. But I mean for the first two or three years he was under control.'

The outcome of their efforts was another also-ran as far as Tony's career was concerned. The critics were not kind. He was to have made another three movies with Associated British Picture Corporation. They never happened. The silver screen, it seemed, was not ready to accommodate Hancock's humour.

Tony's parting with Ray Galton and Alan Simpson presented them with an undreamed-of opportunity.

Tom Sloan, head of BBC TV Variety, asked them what they wanted to do. Ray Galton remembers: 'We said we'd like to write a series with Frankie Howerd and he said, "Oh no, no, no, no, you can't do that." We said "Why? We think he's a great comedian." And he said, "No. No, no, no, he's not popular at the moment." He had his secretary bring in all the charts to prove Frankie Howerd wasn't popular at that time, which indeed he wasn't.

'Tom Sloan offered us a series called *Comedy Playhouse*. He said, "This is my title. I insist on keeping that title, but you can write what you like. You can direct it, you can produce it, you can be in it, you can do anything you like."'

Beryl Vertue put it this way: 'This was the first time – and probably the last – we've ever seen writers' names as part of the title. This demonstrated, quite cruelly from Tony Hancock's point of view, the strength of Galton and Simpson.'

'So,' said Ray Galton, 'we wrote the first two episodes of *Comedy Playhouse*. One of them was called *The Offer*. Tom Sloan said, "Well, you know what you've done here?" "No, er..." "Course you do," he said, "it's a series." We said, "No, no, no, no, the last thing we want to do after working for Tony for ten years or thereabouts, is a series."'

They had written over 100 radio shows and more than 50 TV episodes for Tony.

'We had this amazing freedom to do exactly what we liked, and we were the stars – it was our name and everything else. So we said no for about six months and we found all the excuses under heaven to say why we wouldn't do it. In the end we ran out of excuses and said, "If Harry H. Corbett and Wilfred Brambell want to do it, we'll do it." They jumped at it. We didn't think for one moment they would, but they did.'

Galton and Simpson had concocted the only series to ever assault the pinnacle of nationwide popularity attained by *Hancock's Half-Hour*. Ray Galton freely admits that Harry H. Corbett's character in *Steptoe and Son* was a variation on Tony's *Hancock's Half-Hour* persona.

No amount of cajoling from the BBC could change Tony's mind about mending fences with his alter egos, Galton and Simpson. Tony claimed his character had become moribund, exhausted. Even Sid James tried to persuade Tony to think it over. He wouldn't budge.

Tony retained Philip Oakes as a script consultant, but when he ignored Oakes' advice about using below-par scripts and declined his ideas for a second movie, Oakes resigned. Tony approached another talented guy, Terry Nation – who later created the Daleks for *Doctor Who* – to write material for his stage show, but Tony didn't, perhaps couldn't, come to terms with the material and he reverted to his old routines – or were they chestnuts? – from his archive. Nation accompanied Tony on tour and gradually the new material began to work.

Tony wasn't so lucky with his Independent Television series, which swiftly faded into obscurity. Tony asked Galton and Simpson for help, but it was too late – they had surpassed themselves with *Steptoe and Son*, which consistently featured in the BBC's top ten programme ratings.

Bernard Delfont offered Tony a stint at the Talk of the Town, a prestigious West End theatre restaurant. An insecure Tony backed out and Joan Turner replaced him.

A floundering Tony was beginning to realise how much he needed Galton and Simpson. He made some commercials, discussed many schemes with friends like Spike Milligan and Denis Norden. He even toyed with the idea of playing The Fool to Wilfred Lawson's King Lear, but no one would risk backing a theatre production with a couple of lushes in the leading roles. Protracted negotiations for Tony to star in a movie version of Ionesco's *Rhinoceros* bit the dust.

How deeply he was affected by all this is a matter of conjecture. It is certain that he was drinking heavily. Freddie Ross became his mistress. For his first wife Cicely, it had been a nightmarish relationship. Reconciliation after reconciliation was attempted with Cicely, to no avail. Tony had met her at the Queens Ice Rink in Bayswater, but quite what Tony was doing there remains a mystery. Those who knew Cicely admired her for her patience with Tony. She was a beautiful, attractive woman who ensured that Tony and his visitors to their home were always well fed and watered. She knew how to stay away when Tony was working with colleagues or reminiscing with his cronies.

It was not like that when they were alone. His drinking precipitated enormous rows. When she married Tony, Cicely seldom touched alcohol. She had started drinking more or less in self defence on the 'If you can't fight 'em – join 'em' basis.

As their alcohol intake escalated, so did their arguments, which became increasingly violent physically but nowhere nearly as damaging as the booze. A little over six months after Tony's suicide, Cicely, by then also a chronic alcoholic, died. She was 38 years old.

In 1964, Tony topped the bill in the television show *Sunday Night at the London Palladium*. This received the highest viewing figures of the week and, it seemed, his very ordinary performance partially restored his waning confidence, but it didn't stop the frustration or the violence developing between him and Freddie Ross.

In 1965 he went to the States where he was offered a choice role in a Disney movie called *The Adventures of Bullwhip Griffin*. Tony was to portray a Shakespearean actor caught up in the California Gold Rush of 1849.

Alone in Hollywood and left to his own devices, he was bored. He turned to the vodka and an affair with the wife of a British actor living in the same hotel.

'He thought he fell in love all the time, you see,' one of his friends told me, 'he was monstrously selfish and there was no room, it was Tony and a bottle, really, there wasn't room for anybody else.

'He liked women around to look after him and mother him,' this friend continued, 'I mean, I remember when we were filming there was some little local beauty queen who had landed on him, and she stayed with him all night and she emerged in tears and desperate in the morning. I got her into a taxi when certain people weren't around... She said, "He never touched me, honest. Honest." And I believed it, absolutely.'

Hugh Stuckey says, 'He may have dabbled, but it would have been more a flirtation than anything.'

Freddie flew to LA. Tony pitched up at the studio half-sozzled and saturnine. The Americans weren't as tolerant as the sentimental Brits. He was replaced.

This was a tragedy for him because the film was hailed as 'A rather splendid spoof Western with careful attention to detail and comedy pointing, well above the average Disney standard.'

Hancock flew to Paris to lick his wounds. He was a Francophile and went there as frequently as he could, not only because he relished the anonymity he enjoyed in foreign countries but he delighted in their superb food. And drink. Although he adored good wine and considered himself an expert on the subject, his hard-drinking preferences were brandy and vodka.

Back in London, Bernard Delfont had kept the *Talk of the Town* offer open and Tony did a six-week gig there, still relying on his dusty, ancient material.

Delfont made Hancock another offer. *Noah*. This was a stage musical composed by Leslie Bricusse and adapted from André Obey's play by no less a duo than, yes, Galton and Simpson.

Bricusse thought their script was wonderful. 'You know who you've written this for?' he asked Galton and Simpson, 'It's Tony Hancock – every word. Every word is Tony Hancock.'

'We weren't thinking of Tony Hancock,' they said.

Bricusse said, 'Wouldn't it be wonderful if he could do it?'

'Well no,' they said, 'it wouldn't. He's out of his mind. He hates the stage. He loathes the stage. He can't sing. He's pretty far gone.'

'Would you mind if I showed it to him?'

Galton and Simpson said, 'By all means.'

Tony flipped over it. He too thought it was wonderful. He couldn't wait to do it.

Ray Galton remembers the outcome: 'We were to meet at Bertorelli's restaurant, and we were waiting there. Unbeknown to us Tony had called the Press and he didn't turn up. One o'clock. Two o'clock. All the Press had gone by then, and he eventually turned up with Sean Kenny, who was to do the sets. And that lovely actor drunk – Wilfred Lawson. The three of them out of their minds. That was the end of that.'

But people still had faith in him, and Bryan Forbes gave Tony a cameo role in his movie *The Wrong Box*.

By now Cicely's divorce action was granted.

In 1965 Tony visited Australia for the first time on a cabaret tour. On his return to England he married Freddie Ross. Some three weeks later, a few days after Christmas, he entered an alcohol aversion hospital in Hampstead. His marriage to Freddie metamorphosed into an action replay of his marriage to Cicely. Tony was drinking heavily, and there were horrendous confrontations.

Freddie Hancock chronicles the cataclysmic marriage candidly in her book *Hancock*, in which she confesses to five suicide attempts.

The Beeb repeated 19 of his programmes.

In September 1966 Tony was due to perform his one-man show in the Festival Hall. He urgently needed material. Galton and Simpson were approached and turned him down. This was when, after a ten-year silence, he rang Phyllis Rounce in the small hours of the morning to try to get her writers, John Muir and Eric Geen, to work for him. Kenneth Williams was also suddenly remembered because Tony wanted to recreate the famous aeroplane sketch with him. Williams wasn't interested. At the Festival Hall Tony reverted to his tried and true routines ... most of them anyway. The show was nevertheless a success – with the live audience. When the BBC transmitted it, viewers switched off or away. Freddie Hancock wrote: 'It was a travesty of what Hancock had once been.'

In December 1966, he and Freddie parted. The turbulent marriage had lasted less than seven months. A month later, in January 1967, Tony acquired a mistress, Joan Le Mesurier, his best friend John's wife.

For a time they were blissfully happy, but the 'demon drink' still reigned supreme in Tony's life and he kept on drinking, drying out, drinking, drying out, a hideous cycle which included the old drunken violence which is poignantly catalogued in Joan's fascinating, bittersweet book, *Lady Don't Fall Backwards*.

Freddie initiated divorce proceedings against him.

In an interview Tony made a libellous statement about the Delfont Organisation. Billy Marsh despaired of him because of this, his drinking, and in particular his very unprofessional defection from two editions of *The Blackpool Show* television series.

John Collins sensed a deal and persuaded Tony that Australia would be his salvation.

7

The Last Interview

Tony's relationship with Australia was ambivalent. His reputation there was far less sullied than it was in Britain.

Once a member of the crew had called him 'Tone'. I thought he was going to kill the man with one of his scowls. For hours he complained, 'Tone, Tone, bloody nitwit. Tone!'

Apart from this incident, the Aussies held him in great esteem and invariably called him *Mister*, but he was unable to appreciate their warmth and felt ill at ease there, yearning to be back in the UK doing what he was doing in Sydney.

But how did he really see himself? What made him tick? Here, in his own words, is a remarkably frank interview, probably the most revealing since John Freeman's famous *Face to Face*. Russell Clark recorded it in Australia a few months before Tony died.

'My name is Anthony John Hancock. Not Anthony Aloysius, which was dreamed up by my script writers. I am forty-four and I'm out here to make a comedy series for the ATN Channel 7 Network. It will be the first time I have done a television series in colour.

'The series will be an initial thirteen episodes and – I'm not talking in contract terms, but only in terms of what has been discussed conversationally – if everybody is happy, it will certainly go to twenty-six. Then, if it really turns out to be very good, we hope to go to thirty-nine. That doesn't mean I'm considering staying here indefinitely. I couldn't.

44

'But if, after this series goes on, ATN-7 decided they want to do another series, I'd be back over here like a shot.

'There are other things to do. Films, which I'm particularly interested in. Also, after all, the roots are in England and you can't entirely cut them off. I don't really see myself picking up all the sticks and bits and pieces that constitute my possessions and bringing them over here permanently.

'This is a new thing. East Cheam is finished. Dead. Let's drop it with a heavy clang if you like. Permanently.'

We intentionally retained the 'old' Hancock image, the one of the man in the Homburg hat and the coat with the astrakhan collar. Tony knew his trademarks, and was as proud of them as Chaplin was of his cane and bowler hat long after he had abandoned them.

'There is no possibility, not even a remote one that Sid James will come out for an appearance in this series. He's got *George and the Dragon* running for him, so he's okay.

'We're starting something fresh, and, I think, very good. Both script writers are new. The last time I left Australia I'd started working with Hugh Stuckey whom I'd just met, and he wrote two scripts that I liked.

'Then we found Michael Wale, who I'd never met, in England, and Eddie Joffe – and fortunately we fitted. We have the same enthusiasms, attitudes and purpose in mind – to make it run and run and run.

'I think initially it does worry me a little to be working in all this newness. It's important to walk on a set to a crew who are completely known to you and compatible – not that there's been the slightest sign to the contrary, but after a few shows you get to know everybody and the thing becomes a unit. This will happen.

'I was born in Birmingham and my dad was – hah! What wasn't he? He was a boxing referee, a club owner, a pub owner, he owned a laundry. It was a fairly scattered career.

45

Also he was a semi-pro entertainer, doing things like Ladies' Nights – that sort of thing. He too was a comic.'

He, too, was an alcoholic. Jack Hancock died of cancer in 1935, when Tony was 11 years old. His father had dark, sleek hair and was a stage 'toff', appearing as he did, in top hat and tails, sporting a monocle and brandishing a long cigarette holder which became his trademark. His mother, Lillian, remarried eight months later. His stepfather committed suicide at the age of 44 ...

'My brother [Roger] was a performer too – a very reluctant one. He gave it up after two or three times. I had two brothers. The older one was killed in the war. The younger one is a rather pompous type of literary agent who handles script writers. A very wise thing to do.

'At school I was madly interested in sport. I left school when I was about fifteen. It was an English public school which I didn't like at all. Not because of the discipline but because I didn't agree with the principle.

'I got into this entertainment business partly because I thought it meant I could stay in bed in the morning. I found out you can't and you don't.

'It's one of the most highly disciplined businesses. You've got to be there. If I'm on at eight, I can't turn up at five past. We had a man who was always late. One day there was a call at ten o'clock and he arrived at a quarter to one.

'"And what happened to you?" we asked with a sort of quiet, gentle savagery. "We started at ten. We've just had somebody else read your scene for you."

'"Well," he said, "I had a nose bleed on the Morden-Edgware line."

'What can you do with a man like that? We had to forgive him. If you can come up with an excuse like that, Charlie, you deserve to be two-and-a-half hours late.

'The pace of our business has speeded up so much since I came into it. Danny Kaye did us a great deal of harm, we'd always thought that about fifteen minutes was long enough

46

for a comedy spot – and suddenly on comes this gentleman who does an hour and a half.

'This started the tendency for the very long one-man acts, and I think most of us successfully learned to cope with it, although it looked like the Labour Exchange for most of us for a while.

'It's a lonely business. Most actors and artists of all sorts I've met are introverts. You find yourself talking to yourself in the wings. I stand there saying, "Come on, you silly fool. Get your feet down, take it slow and get the feel of what's going to happen."

'I always go into a theatre as the show starts. Usually I take the second half. I do about an hour. I go in early, not necessarily to hear the reaction to the other artists, but there's a sort of sniff about a theatre. You think – hmmm, it seems a little strange tonight – and I'll probably adopt a different tempo to try to fit the audience.

'It's partly true that I'm a lonely person. There are times when you're desperately lonely, standing in the wings at, say, the Palladium – and the music plays and everybody's helped you and everything that can be done has been done. That's isolation. Nobody can help you any more. And I think some of this carries over into your personal life. You're out there alone. To be shot at, shouted at, booed, have rivets thrown at you (which I've had) and sevenpence ha'penny thrown at me at Bristol – which I picked up carefully off the stage and went and bought myself half a bitter.

'How do you make comedy? You don't make it with measured ingredients – it's not a cake. You make comedy with feeling. If there is pathos there, it is there. It's implicit, not put in as an ingredient. A scene should play itself. You see the character on paper, and you get him and you play him.

'All this Method acting is nonsense. If you're going to play, say a docker, you don't go down to the docks and look at them. I'm sure a man like Peter Sellers doesn't do that.

47

'A man I know is one of those experts at playing himself. We were on a show together. Funnily enough, it was about immigration to Australia. I had a huge parrot under one arm and a carpet under the other.

'My line was, "I wish to fly to Australia." His line was, "On the carpet or on the parrot?" He'd been to Australia House and stayed there all day watching the procedure of the whole thing and then came back and, bless his heart, played himself.

'What I play on television is an extension of myself and the idiosyncrasies of other people combined. I'm against playing comedy where you just hit out at certain stupidities of certain people.

'You are, after all, involved in life, and you do certain stupid things yourself. So, if you're going to stand there and throw stones, at what point of perfection do you stand? If one is going to be critical without any chance of comeback, it's like hitting a child.

'I've been criticised. And how I've been criticised. I have kept my worst criticism. I took twelve copies of it back from New York. This may seem masochistic. It isn't. It's a reminder to me that this was once written about me.

'I made a film titled *The Rebel*, and everyone was saying to me that there are nine other critics, but if Crowther of the *New York Times* likes it you're in. He devoted two columns to me which began, "Norman Wisdom can now roll over because England has found an even lower comic." He went on in this vein about the general performance for the first column. Then he said, "BUT, not only is he responsible for the performance, but he is also, I understand from the credits, responsible for part of the script." Then he devoted another column to that.

'I think that in creating comedy the great thing is to live as close as possible to your writers socially. We used to find – Alan Simpson, Ray Galton and I – that most of the good ideas would come from going out and having dinner or something and just chatting generally.

'That's how we made East Cheam and the belligerent, sometimes malicious little man that was me. I wasn't a little man fighting against bureaucracy. This is nonsense. The press always has a tendency to pigeonhole characters. It's wrong. He was always trying to make life a little less deadly than it really is, and a lot of it was extremely belligerent comedy.

'It was, if I may say so, extremely successful. But we reached a point at which it was becoming progressively more difficult to write. We'd exhausted the situations we could do, so we dropped it.

'It's no good entertaining your audience for a while then boring them, because the sum total is to leave a bad taste.

'I'm not in this business only to pick up a pay cheque every week. Initially, of course, you want to go on there and have the lights turned on you, and think This Is Me and the ego is bursting out all over you. But after a while you begin to get into the depth of it. It's a tremendous challenge and an exciting and very frightening way of making some sort of existence for yourself, and ... and you become isolated.'

8

'How is he behaving?'

The first read through on Easter Monday, 15 April 1968, was a
sizzling success.

Some of the sets had been erected in the main studio and the
designer had dressed them (i.e. added all furniture, drapes and
props) for me to see. It looked good. Tony's 'home base' set, his
apartment, was exactly right, complete with flying ducks, a print
of Tretchikoff's *Chinese Lady* and cheap, kitsch furniture, reflecting, as it was supposed to, the landlady's appalling bad taste.

The ambiance was sublime. The unexpected pleasure of seeing
the sets *in situ* so far in advance of the recording, and better still,
being able to rehearse in them, had a profound effect on Tony
who, at last, felt 'at home' doing what he did best. He had studied
the script meticulously and gave, what we all agreed, was the best
Hancock performance anyone had yet seen. Tony, script in hand,
was relaxed, confident, and in top form. He was enjoying himself
to the nth degree, hamming away to the utmost of his great ability,
in what was almost a parody of himself. His flamboyant performance was way over the top, but he had his audience – the cast
and members of the crew – in stitches.

One of the prime objectives of a first read-through is for all
concerned, cast and crew, to get the 'feel' of the production.

Normally only key technicians are rostered to attend, but many
members of the crew who were not scheduled for duty that day
turned up, wanting to see the great Tony Hancock in action. The
Hancock name not only attracted almost a full crew complement

After discovering that the hotel is overcharging, Tony restores the balance by purloining a few items (© Seven Network – Australia)

Tony contemplates the hotel maid's ad⋯ ⋯pril 1968, with j⋯1 web spiders (© Seven Network – Australia)

Location Polaroid continuity still. 'Bon' as in 'Bondi'

A rare picture of Tony on a social outing in Sydney ...offe (near right) and friends Ron and Doreen Lambert.

to the session, but also quite a number of ATN-7 staff who had nothing whatever to do with the series. And this was on an Easter Monday public holiday. They were well rewarded for their trouble with a priceless performance from Tony acting his socks off.

Tony's cast responded marvellously. They were on the verge of participating in Hancock's comeback, actively contributing to a comedy performance second to none.

Everyone left the read-through exhilarated and filled with optimism that Hancock was in his best-ever form and that we had an absolute winner on our hands!

The following day the studio was unavailable for rehearsals. Nor was there any rehearsal space at ATN-7's Epping studio complex, so a hall had been rented in a squalid part of suburban Sydney. On arrival we were told we could only use this tacky dump until lunchtime since someone had double-booked the venue, which meant we had to try to find an alternative in a hell of a hurry.

Tony had been on a high from the success of the previous day's read-through, where all present, including the cast, had enthusiastically and spontaneously applauded his virtuoso performance. He had obviously celebrated his triumph that evening and arrived at rehearsals somewhat the worse for wear, his buzz dissipated by booze.

The difference between the rehearsal and the read-through was beyond belief. 'By the end of the week, rehearsals were just a dreary, sitting-about drag,' Clare wrote, 'while the producer sat and talked and cajoled Hancock into uttering a few slurred lines of the script.'

Tony clutched his script tightly, reading the lines as if it were the first time he'd seen them and delivering them like an automaton. The rest of the cast were almost word-perfect. We persevered until the lunch break. Tony and the cast departed. Clare and I settled for a sandwich and checked some production details while awaiting a phone call from our production office about the new venue for the afternoon's rehearsals. Of course this gave Tony time to kill – and where better to do so than the nearest tavern.

51

By the time an alternative room was found we salvaged what was left of Tony from the bar where he had become their most celebrated customer ever. He was staggering drunk and couldn't see his script, let alone read it. I asked him if he wanted a rest.

'No,' he retorted, 'I want a bloody drink.' And off he tottered to find another boozer.

That evening Tony rang me several times to tell me about his discovery that day of a phenomenon known as the 'six o'clock swill'. The liquor laws in Melbourne had once dictated that bars had to shut at 6 p.m. and as work finished at 5.30, the customers lined up as many beers as they could swill down before closing with the result that the bars became vomitoria. Publicans had been forced to tile everything – the floors, the counters, the walls to a height of six feet – the lot – in order to hose it all down at closing time. Being cheapest, brown tiles were always used. One of the bars Tony had graced that day had followed the Melbourne tradition and still boasted these tiles. Tony wanted me to call for him so that he could show me this 'fine example of Australia's magnificent past' which had survived the bulldozers.

After the expectations kindled at the read-through, this day proved a tremendously harsh experience and we were all too shattered to even talk about it. I had no choice but to cancel that rehearsal.

On the third morning Tony further demolished our ever-dwindling hopes for the series by again arriving stoned. His speech was incomprehensible as he struggled to focus on his script. Because he featured in every scene in the show, there was no point in continuing the charade so I released the supporting cast. I determined to somehow get him to the starting line in as good a shape as possible.

It hadn't been an easy day for anyone, particularly Clare. 'Hancock expressed a strong dislike of the colour green, for superstitious reasons, which,' she wrote home, 'since the production is in colour, presents considerable last-minute complications. I appeared at rehearsal in my green trouser suit and if he said, "You look lovely, darling, but don't wear green" once, he said it a dozen times.'

The next day – Thursday – was to be the final dry (outside) rehearsal, and I insisted he accompany me to my hotel that evening for a meal.

The staff at Tony's hotel, the Georgian House, had reported that when he was on his own he hardly ate anything and most of his meals had been a hundred per cent liquid. My naïve expectation was to try to get some food into him in the hope that a good meal would somehow help keep him sober.

Coincidentally, the subtitle of the first programme to be recorded was 'Sleepless Nights'. It proved appropriate and gave me nightmares as well, but, I persuaded myself, since we were filming as opposed to videotape recording, and because there was no audience, I thought it might be possible to manage 'on the day' using cue cards and film techniques instead of the planned multi-camera method.

At our very first meeting, Tony and I had made a pact in which we pledged that if one of us had a grievance either creatively or personally, we would be honest and open with one another and speak our minds. In private. Under no circumstances, we had agreed, would we vent our feelings or argue in front of the cast or crew. I determined to put our agreement to the test that evening.

When we reached my hotel I told him that we would both be in very deep trouble unless he arrived sober at rehearsals the next morning. Again I reminded him of a warning I'd given him the previous night – that it wouldn't be long before someone alerted the Press about his behaviour.

The local Press, or most of it anyway, wanted him to succeed and were very kind to him. They tended to play down the Melbourne stage incident, and although they didn't want to cry doom, they had to sell newspapers.

ATN Channel 7, Sydney, was owned by the Fairfax newspaper group. Understandably they did not want their expensive star's drinking secrets spread over rival front pages. They didn't need the sort of adverse publicity that Hancock's addiction would inevitably elicit. I was acutely aware of their misgivings but I had no idea of how to handle the situation, having only encountered one alcoholic before Tony Hancock. I wanted Tony to know that he was seriously endangering the possibility of the series continuing and that he stood a better than average chance of drinking himself to death.

I told him the story of a folk singer and entertainer I'd once worked with called Alex Campbell, who happened to be the man Billy Connolly chose as the role model for his early career. Like Tony, Alex also had a touch of genius and a weakness for alcohol. When Alex had emptied his bottle of Scotch to a certain level his performances were nothing short of superb. Too little or too much, and he was terrible. Alex's problem was that the invisible level on the bottle kept changing, and he never did find out exactly where that magic level was before he died of cirrhosis of the liver.

Little did I know that Tony was already suffering from liver problems.

Tony accepted that what I was saying was for his own good, and he listened in silence, a hangdog expression on his face, until I finished. My relationship with him had shifted from that of worshipful acolyte to severe schoolmaster. I'd fully expected him to take umbrage at what I said, but he admitted that he realised I was trying to stop him from destroying himself. Then he launched into a long spiel of how much he disliked Oz, its people in general and John Collins in particular.

Why, he wanted to know, didn't we return to England and make the series there? My answer was that it was clearly out of the question for a number of reasons, not least of which was the fact that no one would touch him in the UK unless and until he quit drinking. He nodded agreement.

That night was one of the longest I have ever had. I ordered steaks for two to be served in my room. Tony merely picked listlessly at his potato croquettes. He wanted to return to his hotel 'for his pills'. He asked if he could have a glass of wine to wash down his food. As he hadn't imbibed for some hours and was beginning to tremble, I didn't think wine would be nearly as harmful as spirits, so I had a bottle sent up.

Clare wrote home: 'I went from work to the producer's hotel room to collect information from him for the 'morrow. Hancock was there, dining with him in his room. No sooner did I come in,

54

than the poor man (Hancock that is) staggered into the bathroom and was violently sick – so I really thought it was me! – in my green trouser-suit too! He is desperately pathetic, but, alas, the undoubted talent he once had has evaporated with the alcoholic fumes into the air. Now he is just a pathetic, mumbling, red-eyed person who has to be led, coaxed and pushed through any scene he performs.'

Tony talked, how he talked that night. All his doubts and insecurities tumbled out, and I realised just how far gone he was psychologically.

That night in a Sydney hotel, he sketched out some touching incidents of his life. He spoke at great length about his deep affection for his older brother Colin – a tall, slim, charming and charismatic young man – whose plane had crashed in the English Channel during the last few months of the war. His body was never recovered and Tony claimed that Colin's spectre regularly appeared to him in dreams, swathed in seaweed.

Tony was alone and very lonely. My heart bled for him. He was pining for Joan. When I asked why he hadn't brought her with him for company, he mumbled that the relationship had to be kept secret because his impending divorce from Freddie was causing him insurmountable difficulties and he, Joan and his solicitors were anxious that she be kept out of the proceedings for fear of her being cited as co-respondent.

It was too late because Joan had, in fact, been shadowed by a private detective and had been named in Freddie's petition. Tony was advised not to defend the case because the petition had not spared any detail of Tony's life style, including his drunken nights, his violence, her suicide attempts and his sexual preferences. In those days, anything other than the missionary position was regarded as deviant behaviour. Any one of these factors may well have ruined his reputation if publicised, but the combination would have been lethal. It nevertheless took a lot of persuasion to get a very stubborn Tony to agree to the solicitors' advice

I went to a cupboard for some cigarettes. Inside were a few bottles of duty-free Scotch which Tony's radar uncannily detected. He asked, almost humbly, if he could have a whisky. Having

55

already deprived him of his pills I felt it would be pointless to refuse him. I knew that if he insisted on leaving I wouldn't be able to stop him.

I also knew that if he returned to his hotel and was alone he'd certainly indulge in another all-night drinking session which would effectively put paid to the next day's rehearsals, so I poured him a small tot, imagining I'd be able to control his intake. I didn't care much for Scotch, but I felt the only thing to do was give him the impression that I was matching him drink for drink, the idea being that the more I emptied the bottle, the less there would be for him to consume. Two decades later I heard that Cicely had used the identical technique. It hadn't worked for her either.

Between repeated requests to return to his hotel for pills and gulps of whisky, he talked at length about his marriage to Freddie Ross, with whom he had fallen out of love in less time than it had taken him to bed her in the first place. He couldn't stand her, he said. Nor could he explain why he'd married her. He claimed she'd married him for business purposes to enable her to bask in his reflected glory.

Her suicide attempts amused him. He revelled in relating a distasteful story of how she had accidentally taken a handful of laxatives instead of her sleeping pills. 'Didn't get a wink for two days,' he gloated.

His only concern about his divorce from Freddie was the possibility of her getting her hands on most of his money in the divorce settlement. He wasn't worried about money for his own sake, but he was anxious to ensure there'd be enough left to take care of his mother. Tony loved, respected, indeed doted on his mother. He felt totally responsible for her welfare, and one of his obsessions was that she should never lack for anything.

He assured me that not only was she his mother, but also his best friend and confidante. There had never been any secrets between them, he said. They used to discuss golf and cricket. Those who knew them say they were like a comedy act together, ribbing each other, with Tony teasing her about her food foibles. Beryl Vertue remembers her as being very, very amusing and down to earth. Tony was very much a mother's boy, through and through. To me it seemed he had a fixation.

He suddenly picked up the phone and barked: 'Get me Bournemouth.' When he was connected to his mother there, he talked to her for a few minutes before insisting I speak to her as well.

'How is he behaving?' she asked, as if he were a ten-year-old child. I told her he wasn't behaving well and that she should talk some sense into him. Mrs Sennett thanked me for all 'the help and support' I had given Tony. She told me how she worried about him having to cope with so many problems at work (Tony had discussed the Collins affair with her) and his messy divorce. She expressed deep concern about his being lonely and was very pleased, she said, that he had 'someone like me' to turn to. She asked if he was taking his pills (she was referring to his Antabuse, a prescription drug which induces nausea if taken before consuming alcohol). I repeated her question to Tony, who laughed and gave me a double thumbs-up sign, and when Mrs Sennett laughed at what I told her Tony was doing, it was a relief as it meant I didn't have to lie to her since I knew he hadn't taken any that day. While she and I were talking, Tony downed quite a few tumblers of whisky in swift succession.

Too late, I thought, when I realised that the phone call was really a premeditated ploy to divert my attention from guarding the Scotch. After saying goodbye to Mrs Sennett I poured the remnants of the bottle into my tumbler, which I later chucked in a flower vase when Tony went to the loo.

On his return he made a beeline for the cupboard and was into the second bottle before I could blink. I lost patience with him. I swore at him. I pleaded with him not to drink any more. Nothing I said made the slightest difference. I told him the whole world was waiting for him to succeed with this series, but he ignored me and all I could do was impotently watch him pour large Scotches into both our glasses and pretend to sip mine while waiting for an opportune moment to further wilt the flowers. Tony gripped that bottle with white knuckles to prevent any possibility of my confiscating it.

57

The more he drank, the more maudlin he became. He started brooding about Joan and began to weep drunken tears. It was one of the most heartbreaking experiences I'd ever known. He was wallowing neck-high in self-pity. He spoke about his illnesses and how he had no control over his bowels... The haughty Hancock was a myth, his defences were gone. He was as helpless as a baby.

When the subject somehow shifted to metaphysics, the mixture of whisky and wine I had consumed combined with the hour to cause me to doze off intermittently, so I didn't pay much attention to everything he said. He was certainly a seeker, wanting to probe the mysteries of life and death. We never discussed religion, a subject he avoided and which he had self-consciously stuttered through when it was put directly to him during the Freeman interview. But he must have believed in something, because as he lay dying he wrote in one of his suicide notes, 'The soul is indestructible'.

Twenty-five years later, George Fairweather, an old friend of the Hancock family from Bournemouth, showed me a well-worn letter he had received in July 1968 shortly after Tony's death. It read:

'Dear Mr Fairweather

I was sitting for meditation the other evening when I heard Tony Hancock's voice coming through very clearly, saying that *"I thought the only spirits came out of bottles and I am one now."*

It was so vivid I felt I should tell someone so I'm telling you this. Tell anyone it would comfort in any way. *"Tell anyone I love that I'm not blotted out and will see them all again one day."*

I feel that this should not be made public, however, you must do as you see fit.

Yours sincerely KR – a believer.'

George told me he'd been present in Tony's dressing room at the Adelphi where Tony was working with Jimmy Edwards when Tony received the notification to appear in the Royal Command

58

Performance. This is one of the highest accolades any artiste can earn.

'He got very emotional. He put his arms round me and said, "If it hadn't been for you this could never have happened." Which really was true,' said George, 'because I'd started him off in the business. That's what he meant. And then he sat down and poured himself a drink and he said, "If only dad could've been here to see it." I'm not a spiritualist but I believe in the hereafter, so I said, "Don't you think he will be?" Tony said, "Oh don't give me that rubbish, the only spirits come out of bottles." I dropped the subject then. I never told my wife or anybody about it. That's why I was so impressed with this letter because that was the same thing that Tony said to me, "the only spirits come out of bottles." How does one explain that?'

In their books, both Freddie Ross Hancock and Joan Le Mesurier mention Tony's conversations with his deceased father.

'He used to imagine that he was in spiritual touch with him. It was weird,' Joan related. 'Tony was talking to me as if it was his dad. And he was saying, "Look after him." It was as if his father was talking through him. And he was patting me on the shoulder and saying, "He's a good man. He needs help."'

It seems Tony planned to write a book on an obscure concept he had about man's mortality and immortality, to be entitled *The Link*. Apparently he used to sit at his desk with this piece of paper that read 'The Link, by Tony Hancock'. Then he'd add '...or Anyone For Tennis?' And that's as far as he ever got with it.

That long night in the Sydney hotel wasn't entirely harrowing, and when I manoeuvred the conversation around to his early career, he cheered up and talked about how he had once shared accommodation with Spike Milligan who slept under the grand piano because he felt that was where he belonged. Tony attributed Spike's success to the brain damage he suffered by frequently banging his head on the bottom of the piano whenever he forgot where he was when he woke up.

I tried to persuade Tony to tell me about his relationships with Sid James and Galton and Simpson, because I wanted to know why he'd elbowed them and so many others who had helped him along the road to stardom.

Joan said, 'I think he was rather embarrassed about his treatment of Sid, because Sid was terribly hurt about being ditched by him.'

Maybe this was the reason Tony refused to be drawn on a personal level and limited his comments to his professional relationship with Galton and Simpson, claiming they didn't sit down to write and have to invent everything. He maintained they would stand with him at the bar for hours on end, just listening to him talk, after which they would utilise much of what he had said, fine-tuning it as they wrote.

He said, for example, that their inspiration for *The Blood Donor*, arguably one of their most outstanding scripts, was based on an accident he'd had which landed him in hospital. Ray Galton found all this amusing when I discussed it with him. He said that every-thing he and Alan Simpson wrote was original. He put it like this: 'Tony was brilliant, but he never contributed one word to the scripts and the only time we sat around to discuss anything was for the films.'

Alan Simpson elaborated: 'The character developed over the years. When you listen to the original *Calling All Forces* and the original *Hancock's Half-Hour*s in 1954, Tony's performance was totally different. It was still left over from *Educating Archie*, as if he were playing the headmaster, Archie's tutor – "Oh hello, hello my little wooden friend." Gradually Ray and I wrote the Hancock charac-ter in Hancock's image, so the Hancock character is not Tony himself – it's a character created in Tony's own image. It sounds like Tony. In the end he wasn't acting, he was playing himself.'

I had been told that Tony abruptly parted company with almost all his friends and colleagues who had contributed so much to his TV and radio shows because many of them became stars in their own right and Tony resented their success.

Ray Galton and Alan Simpson took a more charitable view. 'When he split with Sid [James],' said Galton, 'Sid had a career outside of Tony Hancock. Sid made more films than anybody in the country. I think Hancock didn't resent it, but he was certainly aware of it.'

Alan Simpson: 'Getting rid of the old – Hattie [Jacques] for

60

instance – and Ken Williams from the radio show – it was a professional decision. I agreed with that. The point with Sid was that Tony felt it was becoming a double act, another Laurel and Hardy which wasn't what he wanted. Wherever he went people would say, "Where's Sid?" It was almost as if he couldn't work without Sid. Tony always had this ambition to be international, and by being a double act he couldn't see it developing, and he decided that he would get away from criminality and all that business we'd done over the previous series, so that Sid wasn't a crook so much as just his mate.'

In the first show of the next series Tony was entirely on his own. It was called *The Bedsitter*.

'So,' said Galton, 'he just thought that he'd have a go and do something on his own. Tony kept saying, "We can do better", which is very nice except he had no idea how we could do better. He was moving – moving away. That was why we moved him out of East Cheam. It was too parochial. That was another move. He dropped everybody else, so we dropped East Cheam and he was on his own for the last series.'

Alan Simpson: 'People will say to you now – after all these years, "Well, I don't think he's the same without Sid." And we say, "Well, what about *The Blood Donor*?" "Oh yeah, forgot about that, yeah." "*Radio Ham*?" "Oh yeah, forgot about that." "*The Lift*?" "Oh, wasn't Sid in that?" All the shows Tony's remembered for were all without Sid – *The Radio Ham. The Blood Donor. The Lift*. They were all in the last series of six. Sid wasn't in any of those. People still have this thing about how he gradually got rid of everybody. It was professional. It wasn't jealousy or anything like that – it was professional.'

Beryl Vertue felt: 'The one thing that I think he seriously did need was Galton and Simpson. So that was not only a very bad personal decision on his part, because they had fun together. They were really, really good together, but from a commercial point of view it turned out in more ways than one, to be a suicidal decision, because that's what it led to, I think.'

Joan Le Mesurier: 'His ego got so enormous he thought he could do without them.'

61

Actress Liz Fraser, an 'old mate' of Tony's, recalled his telling her: 'It's not me – I'm not good. It's the writing that's good.'

I'd taken the precaution of asking the hotel night staff to ensure that if Mr Hancock ordered alcohol to be sent to my room he was to be told that the bar was shut for the night and that the keys were not available. Inevitably, when I went to the bathroom, Tony rang down but the staff stuck to the script. So he ordered coffee. This stimulation set him off on another introspective monologue. By then I had started to feel like a captive priest in a confessional, and I was very tired and beyond hearing anything. I often wonder what I would have learnt if I'd been able to stay awake.

As the night dragged on and on he spoke on and on about his doubts and insecurities. I was exhausted and begged him to get some sleep, but he said, 'I can't do that, I haven't got my pills with me.' Nevertheless, at about three – or it may have been four – in the morning he ran out of gas and crashed on the sofa. I staggered to the bed and was out for the count in a nanosecond.

I felt like hell in the morning, but at least Tony'd had a pill-free evening and a mere fraction of his usual alcohol consumption. The long night had paid off, and we actually rehearsed the entire show despite the fact that Tony still had his script in hand while his supporting cast were all word-perfect.

9

'Too weary and bewildered to weep'

The most important shows in any series are usually episodes one (the establisher) and two. These have to be strong enough to attract an audience and to acquire approval from reviewers and critics. If they like the first few programmes viewers tend to stay with the series, and are generally prepared to forgive the odd show which may not be quite up to expectations.

I felt relatively safe shooting Episode Six first. It was chosen because it was the simplest of all the completed scripts. Although it was labelled Number 6, it could have been screened anywhere in the transmission order after Number Three. Episode Six could, if necessary, be 'lost' among better shows.

Tony was far from ready for filming on Friday 19 April. The thought of those humiliating, abandoned rehearsals must have considerably undermined whatever confidence may have survived, and it was no surprise that he did not exactly sparkle on his first day in the studio. The fact that he had reported for duty sober was itself an unexpectedly pleasant event. Compared with the travesty of rehearsals his performance didn't seem too bad. Every now and then, there was an almost subliminal glimpse of the 'old' Hancock, and it was this which helped restore a modicum of optimism. Admittedly my comforter was my knowledge that if the episode was below standard for any reason, ATN-7 had agreed to a re-shoot. After all, I had stressed to them that the rush to get Tony in front of the cameras had not exactly boosted his morale. Unquestionably more preparation time would have helped.

There were a lot of extras in the studio, which was a blessing because Tony was able to pace his performance on their response to him as his audience.

At the end of the first production day we wrapped on schedule and left for home relatively happy. Our supporting cast had turned in fine performances and had managed, without much effort, to upstage Tony on several occasions.

In among the few flashes of brilliance in some of his lines that day, a lot of laughs were harvested, particularly from a cinema scene in which Tony, as a latecomer, disturbs all the other patrons. In the dark Tony misses his seat and lands on the lap of a very large man. Once settled in his own seat, he finds it difficult to see the screen so he taps the person in front of him.

'Pardon me,' says he, 'but would you mind removing your hat, madam?' When the person turns round, Tony realises it's a turbaned Sikh. 'Oops, sorry,' Tony apologises, 'I hope your head gets better soon.'

The usherette appears with her ice cream tray. Tony's antics again annoy almost everyone as he orders a paddle pop, some peanuts, crisps and a Violet Crumble. The big guy on whose lap Tony had sat loses patience and tries to lift Tony bodily back to his seat, but strong as he is, he hadn't bargained on Tony being quite so heavy and it takes him several goes at it before he eventually succeeds. Everyone except the big guy enjoyed the retakes.

On the first studio day we completed all the scenes involving actors and extras. Day two was to be devoted entirely to Tony's solo sequences.

His nocturnal activities brought him to the studio in a deplorable state. The thought of the ordeal that awaited him, under-rehearsed and alone, in front of the cameras must have preyed on his mind. He had taken his usual morning hair of the dog 'steadier', then washed down some pills with another drink, after which he'd popped a tranquilliser to counteract the drink, then a stimulant or two with a slug of vodka to counteract the tranquilliser... It was a hideous vicious circle which had transformed Tony into a walking pill bottle.

Alcohol kills brain cells. If you drink in moderation, you won't miss the odd cell or two. But, according to the doctor who later treated Tony, excessive drinking destroys cells in profusion, and these cells cannot be replaced. What wasn't known then, since it was only discovered in a 1997 research study, was that alcoholics who are 'drying out' produce high levels of chemicals that can kill brain cells. To quote the *Times* report: 'The more often a person has dried out and then relapsed, the more likely it is that he has brain damage.' No one knows quite how many dozens of sessions Tony underwent, but his superlative, instinctive timing had seriously deteriorated. Sid James was quoted as saying, 'I've never known better timing.' Tony and I had discussed timing at length, but arguing with him when he was full of booze and tablets was a pointless exercise as he continued to believe that his timing was as perfect as ever.

Regrettably it wasn't. His performance was well below standard. Each time the cameras rolled, Take One was always best. It was not necessarily good, but no matter how many re-takes we shot, Take One was the one. He was unable to 'build' on previous takes, and even when we re-shot anything because of some technical glitch, we invariably used the technically imperfect take in the end.

It was a nightmare of a morning, and prophetically the subtitle of the show we were working on was *Sleepless Night*. In it, Tony suffers from insomnia, but it may as well have been amnesia... He staggered about the studio and even fell asleep on set a few times between takes.

Sleepless Night begins with Tony trying to get to sleep by counting sheep. The script went like this:

Bedroom   Night   Lights off
'Two thousand nine hundred and thirty-three ... two thousand nine hundred and thirty-four ... two thousand nine hundred and ... Allez oop – I'll have you for mutton if you don't watch it, come on, come on ... two thousand nine hundred and thirty-five ... two thousand nine hundred and thirty-six ... two thousand nine hundred and thirty-seven.'

65

Tony crawls along the bed and imitates a sheepdog. He growls and snaps at imaginary sheep. Wriggles on his stomach and then gets back between the sheets.

'Watch it. Watch it. One false move and I'll snap you in half... It's no good. I can't get to sleep. Whoever thought up this thing of counting sheep anyway? Must have been a vegetarian butcher. Why not count duck-billed platypuses or rhinoceroses. I lie (he lies down) – rhinoceri?... No, it's no good. Perhaps reading might help. A dip into the bountiful knowledge of the cosmos around us never did anyone any harm... Where's that *Digest*?'

He fetches up a *Reader's Digest* from a dressing table. He takes a puff of his cigarette and puts it in an ashtray on the floor beside the bed, next to his slippers. He scans the cover of the *Digest*.

'No doubt about it, the best three bob's worth of culture outside of *Mad* magazine.'

He absent-mindedly uses his slipper on the floor as an ashtray.

'The editor of this magazine must be the world's greatest hypochondriac. I bet his office is just like a surgery.'

He puts the half-finished cigarette in his slipper instead of the ashtray next to it on the floor.

'Oh, I've got to get to sleep. I'm dying. I'm so tired.'

He turns off the lights, lies down and closes his eyes. We hear the rhythmic dripping of a tap. He blinks in rhythm. Every time he hears the drip he opens his eyes.

'Hot chocolate, drinking chocolate, hot chocolate, drinking chocolate. Hot chocolate ... hot chocolate?'

He sits up, turns on the light.

'I must be going stark raving mad!'

He hears more drips. Reluctantly he gets out of bed, takes gown, puts arm in sleeve, puts foot in smouldering slipper. Reacts as if foot is burnt. He hobbles towards the door.

Kitchen   Night   The lights go on
Dripping tap. Smouldering slipper (by now exaggerated) into

66

shot. Tony turns tap on, extinguishes slipper, turns tap off. Looks with grim satisfaction to see drips stopped.

Wrings out slipper, makes room for it on plate drying rack and places it there. He turns to go back to bed.

Bedroom   Night   Lights off
Tony grunting quietly in bed, almost asleep. Drips begin again. Tony opens one eye and twitches to rhythm of drips.

Kitchen   Night   Lights on
Tony tries to turn the tap off, but drip continues. He takes a bowl from drying rack to catch them and the note of the drips turns to a high pitch. Disgusted, Tony gives the tap a good big wrench. The head comes off in his hand and the water jets out in full force, mainly into the sink. Tony backs away in fear. He plugs the tap with his finger to avoid a flood and reaches for the telephone on the counter near the sink.

'Man the pumps. Emergency, emergency, emergency. Get the brigade.'

Dials emergency call.

Voice over on filter, 'Fire, ambulance or police?'

'Fire, but have the ambulance standing by.'

The dialogue develops into a cleverly written, typically one-sided Hancockian debate with the emergency service man, who advises him to call a plumber.

At least that's what it said in the script... We modified and improved it at rehearsal, which is where the written words came alive and where we polished his lines as we went along and also worked out and decided between us how the action should evolve, where he would 'work' the facial expressions, where he would move to and so on.

In his condition he could not remember anything agreed at rehearsal. Tony was on autopilot, and only sheer instinct and will-power, rather than physical ability, kept him going.

But the nightmare worsened.

As the morning wore on with retake after retake and nothing

going right, I heard a bird call which continued intermittently for some time. At first I thought it was a member of the crew with a warped sense of humour because each time we started the count-down to a take, this chirping sound began again and we had to abort. We were shooting synchronised interior sound and couldn't continue until the problem was resolved. After several more false starts due to the noise, I stopped filming to investigate the situation.

The studio lighting grid was 40 feet above the floor. Higher still was an access door to the studio roof. This had been left open and a bird, I think it was a swallow, flew into the studio and its chirping was screwing up our filming.

The old music hall gag about how to cook a turkey – first catch the bird – sprang to mind. We couldn't see it, let alone catch it or frighten it away. It seemed to know when we were getting warm and winged silently to a new perch in the grid or the top of the scenery, occasionally tweeting almost confidentially to itself. If we could have filmed the chase it would have been pure Keystone Kops, but each minute that ticked by was costing ATN-7 loads of money and the humour of the event escaped me at the time.

The sound guy turned out to be a keen-eyed bird spotter as well as a crack shot with a catapult. At around his twentieth attempt, he scored a direct hit with one of the hard mothballs he used for ammunition. I can't remember if he killed it or not, but the chirping stopped.

Clare Richardson's contemporary perspective differs from mine: 'The whole studio stopped to chase a little swallow,' she wrote. 'The whole of this great colour studio is lined with silver for more light, and there we were, running along the catwalks by the silver roof, chasing the poor little bird, while the director bellowed from the floor, "Don't bother about catching him. I want a corpse and quick." But it was an hour before some David took up a sling (from props) against this mini-Goliath, and shot him, as he sat, with a mothball.'

'I was standing by the director, who was now on the catwalk. "There goes your corpse," I said, as the dead bird fluttered down to the studio floor. I remembered that God is aware of every bird that falls to earth, and felt sure our idiot enterprise was not worth the death of a swallow.

'The death of a man, too. Slowly, agonisingly, the recording was completed, and by ten o'clock the last sequence was shot.'

Tony spent the bird safari in his dressing room. While a whole platoon of grown men tried to frighten this damn bird away and out of the studio, Tony hit the vodka hard before moving on to his Antabuse.

I broke the studio crew for an early lunch intending to re-shoot the tap sequence immediately after lunch.

Tony didn't want any food and promised he'd rest during the break. The fact that he was superstitious, particularly about birds, didn't help relax him. He was, understandably, very depressed by the events of the morning, and he spent the lunch hour again communing with a bottle and rounds of 'uppers' and 'downers'.

The first scene after the break was really quite simple. Any actor, no matter how inexperienced, would have remembered the action and dialogue with ease. Not Tony. He had an intuitive gift of being able to busk and improve the script. When he was sober, that is.

The effect of that chemical cocktail on his mind and body was startling. He was physically present when we restarted, but he had no idea where he was or even who he was for that matter. Despite the safety net of his cue cards, the opiates and alcohol had disconnected his batteries and blitzed his brain. He could barely stand, let alone deliver with those pills sloshing around in the alcohol in his belly.

In short, he was no longer Anthony John Hancock, so much as one of those zombies portrayed in the film *Night of the Living Dead*.

Altogether we tried the scene thirteen times or more. He would either forget to dial a number before delivering his lines or fail to even pick up the receiver before speaking. When he managed the action correctly he'd mouth some half-remembered gobbledygook from some other show he may once have worked on in another life. Whatever he was mumbling bore no resemblance to what was in the script. He couldn't do it – he just couldn't do it.

It was pretty damn obvious to everyone in the studio that all we were doing was wasting our time and Channel 7's money. The huge quantities of strong black coffee we were pouring down Tony's gullet to try to revive him weren't making the slightest difference. At that time I wasn't aware of Tony's other habits – his addiction to amphetamines and barbiturates – and it wasn't until after he died that I found out what drugs Tony was on and deduced what he had been up to that day in his dressing room.

After his death it fell to me to go through his belongings. There was a small airline bag with twenty or more bottles and containers with pills of many colours and hues: barbiturates, benzodiazepines, Antabuse, sodium amytal, you name it.

Philip Oakes remembers the medication Tony took when drying out and slimming for a new series. Tony had fallen into the hands of some 'Awful Doctor Feelgoods' who used to put him in a clinic for a twilight week in which he slept for the whole week. 'The pills he took – the dehydration pills – huge pink things, I mean they were the size of kumquats,' Oakes said, 'Unbelievable. You'd have to use a blowpipe to get one down a horse's throat. He used to get 'em down of course.' 'Dehydration,' Tony told him, 'it's all liquid, it's all water, water retention – get rid of it all.'

Oakes himself took uppers such as dexedrine to get through lengthy work sessions on *The Punch and Judy Man*. Tony said: 'No, no, no, what you want is one of these spansules.'*

'They don't just give you a lift for two or three hours,' Oakes explained. 'They give you a lift for twenty-four hours – so you're awake for twenty-four hours. He didn't warn me that these would keep me awake all this time, so I was absolutely hopping for twenty-four hours.

'He had a doctor in fact who was enchanted by Tony, like all of us were, and the trouble was he prescribed recklessly for Tony, and the pills which killed him I think probably came from that doctor – who was doing him a good turn.'

* Soluble capsules containing coated grains of whatever uppers were fashionable giving a staggered time release.

70

Tony's menu included downers, aka barbiturates or depressants. Taken in moderation with alcohol, the short-term effects of these drugs produce relaxation. The chemicals slow you down. Larger amounts make you more intoxicated and drowsy. Long-term heavy use of barbiturates induces prolonged bouts of intoxication with blackouts, neglect of personal appearance and responsibilities, and personality changes. The drinker suffers episodes of severe depression.

Clearly we were not going to achieve anything by continuing with the filming, but I was not prepared to take the responsibility of abandoning the shoot. I telephoned the Managing Director. He was away somewhere, playing tennis or golf or whatever Australians do on a sunny Saturday afternoon in Sydney. The only executive I could contact was Geoff Healy, Head of Production. I called a break and waited for his arrival. Geoff, an easy-going man if ever there was one, was a former engineer who had risen through the ranks. He wasn't very comfortable with the creative side of production, but I felt it was essential for a senior ATN-7 executive to witness what we were up against because it was so unbelievable. Geoff appeared at about 3.30 p.m. by which time we were more than four hours behind schedule.

He wanted to see Tony at work, so once again the cameras turned over on the telephone sequence. But we weren't due for a miracle. If anything, Tony was worse than ever. It was torture for him and for us. During the five or six takes all Geoff Healy could say was 'Golly' and 'Gee'. We discussed the situation privately and he asked my opinion. I could only repeat what I had told him on the telephone, that we should stop immediately and at least save Tony's sanity, a great deal of time, effort and expensive film stock. I pointed out that everyone was gravely and totally demoralised by the day's grotesque events, and even if we did continue, no one would possibly be able to give of his best.

Healy was most reluctant to sanction my abandoning the shoot. He asked me to try to complete the day's schedule and we would discuss the situation on Monday. I pointed out that finishing was not up to me, but depended on Tony's condition, which had by then deteriorated to the point where he was so lethargic he could hardly walk. Healy shrugged, sighed and left.

The plot called for Tony to take a shower. He is so tired he enters the shower (off screen) in his pyjamas. The shower is heard, then Tony returns to his bedroom soaked to the skin. On the first few takes, the scene crew were very economical with the water.

Clare recorded that: 'By this time Tony didn't have the slightest understanding of what was going on, he was exhausted, defeated, bewildered. He didn't remember that bit of the script; he was just led through the moves with the director yelling, "Now make him wet. I want him really soaked, dripping! Soak him well, now bring him through the door again." And poor Tony was pushed back into shot. The expression of utter bewilderment as he stood there, in the relentless eye of the camera, with water dripping off his hair and down his face, I shall never forget. I left the studio and drove home, too weary and bewildered myself to weep either for the swallow or the man.'

At one stage this bastard director wanted a few words with Tony, who was standing behind a set waiting for yet another cue for yet another take. There he stood, half-drowned, befuddled, rumpled, crumpled.

Tony suffered very badly from stage fright and had to metaphorically flagellate himself to enable him to perform. His right hand twisted the flesh of his left wrist while he berated himself: 'Get out there, you cunt Hancock, get out there and give them a performance. Get out there, you cunt, get out and do this thing,' he repeated, over and over again. For him, acting wasn't a pleasure, it was pure self-immolation. He didn't see me and I didn't want him to know I'd witnessed his misery, so I left without saying anything to him. There was nothing I could say.

In the slipper scene he had wanted to actually put his foot into the smouldering slipper 'for the sake of realism'. It had taken me a while to dissuade him from this futile act, and he only agreed not to do it when I warned him that he'd limp for weeks and would probably be unable to work.

Doubtless a psychiatrist could explain all this. I couldn't, but I could feel his torment.

A journalist once asked me if I thought Tony would have been such a wonderful comedian if he'd been a happy and contented person. I felt then, as I do now, that the answer would have to be no. He was basically a sad man, and if he'd been happy he'd probably never have reached the heights he did. The writer felt I was hedging the question. He said, 'In other words, theatrically, he had to cry in order to make people laugh?' I shrugged my shoulders then, and I do now.

The day had proved most frustrating not only for Tony but for everybody else in the studio. We didn't finish the episode, and when we wrapped everyone left as if we had just attended a funeral which, in a way, we had.

I gave instructions not to process the rushes.

Dusty took Tony back to his hotel.

When I rang Tony later that night to find out how he was, he didn't sound in the least depressed. He asked what I'd thought of the filming. When I said I felt it could have been better, his response was that it was a shame about the business with the bird screwing things up in the studio. He made no reference to his condition or his performance. It was as if nothing unusual had happened that day. I wondered just how much he remembered...

Next day I went to Tony's hotel to see how he was faring. He seemed in a good mood and didn't even mention the previous day. Mike Wale pitched up a little later and we all lunched together, spending the rest of the afternoon discussing ideas for future shows. Tony was impressed with one I suggested in which he would lose his way in a film studio and get locked in the wardrobe department overnight to provide him with the opportunity to indulge in all his tried and trusted repertoire of sketches. He was particularly enthusiastic about this idea since he would not have to make any pretence at learning any lines as he could 'go through the card' in his sleep.

He gave us shorthand versions of a few of his sketches – Johnny Ray, the Budgerigar, Charles Laughton as the Hunchback of Notre Dame and Captain Bligh, the Crooner, and his timeless montage of the characters from the Gaumont British newsreel opening

73

titles. Maybe they were a bit blurred round the edges as was Tony at the time, but they were still very funny indeed. Had he lived and been able to give even a small percentage of his former talent, that episode may well have become a candidate for the Golden Rose award for best comedy at the Montreux television festival. At the very least it would have been a fitting tribute to a great comedian. If only . . .

That evening I had a dinner arrangement with friends. Everyone who knew I was working with Tony would ask when they could meet him, and these friends were no exception. Much to my pleasure and surprise, he accepted the invitation. At the restaurant he behaved as if he hadn't a care in the world. He'd shaved, put on a pressed suit, clean shirt, neatly knotted tie and was perfectly charming, impressing my friends with his anecdotes and the waiters with his friendliness. He even signed a few autographs for other diners, a chore he usually despised. As the evening progressed and the wine wrought its effect, he began to transmogrify into the man he was imitating – Robert Newton as Long John Silver. My friends later told me how appalled and shocked they had been to see him looking so haggard.

On the drive home Tony complained of nausea and was nearly sick in the car. My friends dropped us off to get some air, and Tony swiftly recovered sufficiently to want to 'do' the town.

We were in the famous King's Cross area near a strip joint called The Pink Pussycat, a name that greatly appealed to Tony. He suggested we go in for a drink. The owner, a man who basked in the Runyonesque moniker of Last Card Louie, recognised Tony and instantly made us both honorary members. 'Henceforth,' proclaimed Louie, a suave character of Italian origin, 'henceforth you are an Honorary Tom Cat,' as he presented us each with a card stating that we had been duly admitted to the inner sanctum of The Pink Pussycat. On Tony's he wrote 'Admit free any time courtesy of Last Card Louie'. Doubtless Louie would be flattered to know that Tony was so delighted with this souvenir that he fixed it to the mirror on his dressing table.

By dint of Tony's presence we were served a few schooners of

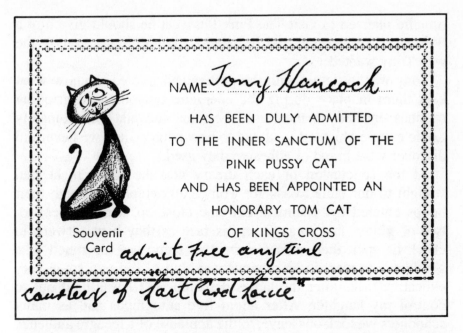

NAME *Tony Hancock*

HAS BEEN DULY ADMITTED
TO THE INNER SANCTUM OF THE
PINK PUSSY CAT
AND HAS BEEN APPOINTED AN
HONORARY TOM CAT
OF KINGS CROSS

Souvenir
Card *admit Free anytime*

courtesy of "Last Card Louie"

beer – an enormous privilege since it was near midnight and it was illegal for them to serve booze after ten. A schooner, incidentally, is three-quarters of a UK pint.

The strippers – Lovable Lolita, Rose Marie from Little Old New York, Carmen the Cat Girl, Gigi, Suzy the School Girl, the Duchess of Peel and others – proved to be dreadfully amateurish. Hardly surprising really, since they were mainly housewives bumping and grinding to earn night-time pin money and allow them to mother small children during the sunshine hours. Tony wished Jack Hylton or Vivian Van Damm could be there to see them.

The slightly misshapen lassies had what appeared to be tinsel sprayed over their nipples. Tony complained to Louie. 'When I come to see tit,' he announced, 'I want to *see* tit.' Louie found this highly amusing and placated Tony by telling him that as a concession to modesty, or it may have been the law, the girls employed devices known as 'pasties' – I think he called them – which were small cones attached to the tips of the mammary glands.

Louie handled Tony with tactful aplomb, assuring him that next time he planned to visit The Pink Pussycat he should give him a little advance warning and he would arrange things exactly the way Tony wanted.

Tony was intrigued with the pasties and wanted to know what kept them in place during the energetic bumping and grinding routines enacted on the raised Formica catwalk. Unfortunately Louie excused himself to attend to new punters, and we never did discover what brand of adhesive they used.

At the conclusion of each dreary act, the strippers headed straight to our table to ask for Tony's autograph. Although their boobs entered his vision in extreme close-up, a mere speck or two of glitter dust away from his face as they bent forward to check he spelt their names correctly, Tony was too much of a gentleman to react in an obvious way, but he did pull some very evocative faces after the ladies departed, and I was hard put to control my laughter. After about five autographs and as many schooners we took our leave, to the applause of a meagre audience of dirty old men as well as the chubby stripper performing at the time.

'I got more applause here than all that time at the Windmill,' Tony muttered as we left.

10

Brand-new gear

The technology we were using, E-CAM (Arriflex's name for their Electronic Motion Picture Film Camera equipment), was an unknown quantity to almost everyone in the Sydney studios. E-CAM has long been obsolete, but in 1968 it was inspired, trailblazing, state-of-the-art technology.

Then, as now, there were three international television standards. Most of the world had opted for the German PAL system. France and a few of her former colonies used the SECAM standard, and the USA adopted its own system – NTSC. Needless to say, the three were incompatible and needed conversion to allow transmission in countries whose line system differed from that of the producing country. Technical conversion standards in the Sixties were nowhere nearly as advanced as they are today. It was also very expensive. Hence the international standard was film, which not only gave a superior quality picture but could be transmitted on all the systems.

E-CAM guaranteed that the technical quality of our shows would be globally acceptable.

Our equipment consisted of three whacking great blimped (soundproof) Arriflex motion picture cameras fitted with integral video viewfinders. Images were recorded on 35-millimetre film in each camera. They incorporated a remote control stop-start gizmo. As shooting methods were more akin to filming than video recording for television, the Hancock series was planned to be shot discontinuously, which meant completing all the action in each set before moving on to the next. This would not have been practical in front of an audience which needs to understand the plot as it moves along. Discontinuous filming does not allow this.

In any case, the space taken up by the sets left no room for a studio audience. Had there been time for my involvement in the early planning, I would have made a strenuous attempt to somehow accommodate an audience, which would certainly have helped Tony gauge his performance and pace it accordingly.

Electronic television demands different techniques. Sitcoms (situation comedy, which loosely includes Tony's show) often have studio audiences. Prior to the arrival of the audience, programmes are rehearsed several times with three or more electronic cameras and then recorded as an entity – 'as live' if you like – in story sequence and, except for technical or artistic fluffs, there are few planned stops and starts.

In film studios there are frequent lengthy breaks between scenes. An audience at our filming sessions would have been unable to follow the plot, and would quickly have lost interest by being subjected to what seems like inordinate time wasting during filming, where everyone appears to stand about apparently aimlessly waiting for Godot while actors rehearse, technicians reload film, adjust camera movements, tinker with the lighting to lose a shadow or eliminate unwanted flare from reflective objects. To the lay observer it looks like nothing is happening. Not so, because somewhere on or off the set, people are beavering away furiously at some particular expertise: sorting out makeup, hair, costumes, props, special effects, what-have-you to get things as near perfect as is humanly possible.

Few technicians on the Hancock show had ever used this equipment before, and we needed all the time we could get to find out what we could or couldn't do with our new toy.

The Australians had themselves experimented with E-CAM on a tennis tournament and a drama, but the latter hadn't been used the way the designers intended – as a multicamera television system.

I had taken a close look at the E-CAM equipment in the UK, courtesy of Mole Richardson who owned the only system in the country. They were exceptionally helpful towards my understanding the technology by letting me see it, view some productions made with it and supplying me with literature and manuals.

I reached Australia with a fair idea of how it operated. Theory is, however, a far cry from hands-on experience of brand-new gear.

In an ideal world, familiarisation time would have been scheduled to test the E-CAM under studio conditions, in order to shake out the gremlins which always seem to breed and proliferate in new machinery. Our schedule allowed two days to record an entire thirty-minute episode which is fairly easy with multicamera videotape TV techniques, but not nearly enough in film terms.

The main drawback with E-CAM was lighting. Multicamera studio-based television productions are almost invariably lit from above. This allows maximum space on the studio floor to enable cameras and microphone booms room to manoeuvre. This type of lighting is best described as 'blanket lighting' – in other words, lighting directors know they will get good quality pictures from almost every camera angle chosen by the director.

During the planning stages of all television productions, the senior camera operator, lighting and sound supervisors, the set designer and the director meet prior to the shoot to discuss camera positions and moves, and the lighting plot is worked out between them to allow for these and for the position of sound booms to prevent shadows being cast on the action or parts of the in-vision set.

In film studios, the lighting is quite different and almost every camera set-up is lit separately. Generally there is only one motion picture camera on the studio floor, and its moves are fine-tuned between the director and the DOP – director of photography – *in the studio* on the shooting day. The result is that there are generally numbers of lamps actually standing on the studio floor, and because the moves are planned, the lamps do not hamper camera movement.

All this is an oversimplification, but it does convey the main difference between the lighting techniques involved in television and film.

My lighting director encountered an unforeseen problem. His lighting grid was old-fashioned and very different from those in the UK in that the Australian scenery had to be positioned in relation to the configuration of the lighting grid, instead of the other way round. Because he had never worked with E-CAM before, his lighting plot was based on his long experience of electronic TV production.

When it was pointed out to him, on the day prior to the first shoot, that the overhead lighting wasn't powerful enough to provide the required minimum for exposure on motion picture stock, he panicked and covered himself by rigging banks of huge, so-called 'soft' lights in various positions on the floor in front of the sets to ensure that the light level was sufficient. These things were some six feet wide and five feet high, not counting their stands. This was done without my knowledge or consent.

For me, creative television production hinges largely on the fluid, unrestricted movement of cameras. The placement of two or three of these damn chunks of lighting hardware in key camera positions restricted the planned manoeuvrability of cameras and microphone booms. Result? Rehearsed artistes' movements had to be adapted to suit lighting requirements, and all my carefully considered shots had to be radically revised on the day, in the studio.

The other complication – the most worrisome – was that the 'soft' lights shone directly into the faces of the actors, half-blinding them. This was bad enough for those who remembered their lines, but it was essential for Tony to see his cue cards, (commonly known as 'idiot boards') and the lights made this very difficult indeed...

So much for pre-planning.

One of E-CAM's chief advantages was that it allowed ultra-fast editing. With electronic studio cameras the switching is instantaneous. Not so with E-CAM. When film is the recording medium, cameras need to run up to the precise speed, which meant that the E-CAM cameras had to be switched on *before* its picture was required for recording. The 'on-air' camera stopped *after* the switch had been made to allow an overlap of 1.5 seconds between every shot. Each time a camera was switched on, dye marks were printed on the edge of the film: one mark for Camera One, two for Camera Two and three for Camera Three. All the editor needed to do was line up the three film rolls side by side and check against the shooting script to determine which camera had been used for the first shot, the second and so on, and match his film against the dye marks. Using this facility, the editing could be completed in a fraction of the time needed to edit in the traditional film method. Thus, by anticipating the switch between cameras, the director dictated the exact cutting point. Although the director seldom physically cuts film personally, E-CAM gave the director total control over the cutting points of continuous action scenes. Even up-tempo musical numbers could be cut to the beat of the music if required. The equipment also offered the more expensive option of running all cameras synchronously to shoot fast action, such as a fight. When used like this, no dye marks were printed and the pictures had to be edited in exactly the same time-consuming way as conventional film.

Obviously the most cost-effective mode, and the one for which E-CAM had been designed, was the multicamera method which made substantial savings on film stock and editing time. The Americans had employed a similar technique on their comedy shows with great efficiency, but the system hadn't gone into general use in the UK because ACTT, the technicians' union, would not allow it. They insisted that the cameras were film cameras and, as such, required four men to operate each one, instead of the one-person operator the Arriflex had been built for. Which is why the equipment never caught on in Britain.

11

'I think we really have a chance'

Tony knew perfectly well that he had fouled his UK nest and that no one there would work with him. John Collins cashed in on this and the knowledge of Tony's burning compulsion to succeed in the United States. As Tony didn't have a whole lot going for him in Britain, Collins had little difficulty in signing him up to make a series in Australia without any reference to Tony's agent, Billy Marsh. Without compunction Tony bypassed Marsh, feeling, correctly, that he would not have agreed to an Australian deal, if only to protect his reputation when the Aussies sussed Tony's condition.

Collins knew that ATN-7 in Sydney was actively seeking projects suited to E-CAM. What with *Hancock's Half-Hour* airing almost simultaneously on two rival Sydney channels, combined with his recent Melbourne stage success, who can blame the Australians for thinking a series starring Hancock was a great idea and that whee – we're onto a winner here. It was this time warp of Tony's fame which clinched the ATN-7 deal for Collins. He didn't do badly because he pocketed 50 per cent of Tony's earnings as well as a fee from ATN-7 for setting up the series.

Ultimately Collins was probably the only person to emerge unscathed from the tragedy. Unscathed and laughing all the way to the bank. I could never squeeze the details of Collins' pay-off from ATN-7, but Tony assured me it was for 26 episodes.

Little did the station know that they were getting a Hancock

These pictures consist of selected 'frames' printed from the working copy of the film to indicate the exact frame to be frozen for the end credits and for the graphic designer to see the precise position of the lettering. (© Seven Network - Australia)

A spot of gourmet–prepared boiled egg

So much for the milk carton...

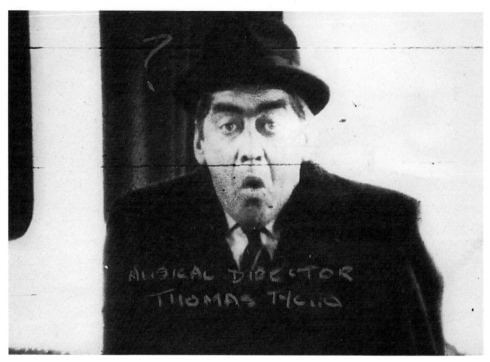

Tony reacting to the effect of the sharp end of a sunshade applied to a tender part of his anatomy

Tony in full cry as a champion jockey

who had blown away his own chances completely and burnt his UK bridges behind him because he was unable to control his drinking.

They were expecting a Hancock who had ceased to exist years before he arrived in Oz. They wanted Hancock the Hero, the man who'd captured a nation's heart and turned a TV series into a legend.

As Ian Moffitt wrote in *The Australian*: 'The real Hancock was the character he portrayed – not the man agonising over a slide from success.'

Tony was determined to prove to those he had rejected, and who he thought had retaliated by rejecting him, that he didn't need them to make it to the top in the USA.

My thoughts were similar to those of the Australians. I knew it was a winning idea. Good scripts. Colour. Film. International market. Blah, blah. All I needed to do was point cameras at a comedy genius and off we'd go together, riding into a Technicolor sunset of television history the easy way...

The cost of 35mm film stock alone was probably higher than the entire budget of an average UK television episode of a similar type and length at that time. The scenery was unquestionably the most elaborate and expensive there had ever been on any previous Australian series.

The sets that had been built or were under construction included, among others, the sun deck of an ocean liner, a ship's ballroom, a huge customs shed with a ship in the background, a cinema interior, an English pub, a hotel lobby, part of a rugby league's club house and of course, Tony's 'home base', an elaborate three-room apartment. These weren't recycled from previous ATN-7 programmes – no sir, these were custom-built.

In short, this series was a very, very big gamble for the Australians.

The writing? It was rumoured that the scripts weren't very good, and it was even hinted that one of the reasons for Tony's suicide was the quality of the scripts. This, in Tony's overworked phrase, was 'a load of codswallop'.

In a letter to Joan he'd stated: 'I think we really have a chance because we are changing the style just that much but it [the series] retains some of the old things but advances without loss to what they have been used to.'

An emasculated video version of the 90-minute special completed after Tony's death found its way into UK video shops. Its dire condition bore the hallmarks of a pirated cutting copy. A cutting copy is a one-off positive, ungraded print made from the film negative and only used for editing purposes. Because it goes through various machines time and time again, it is invariably scratched and worn, and *never* screened outside the editing rooms. When the cutting copy has been honed to everyone's satisfaction, it becomes known as a 'fine cut'. This is precisely matched against the virgin negative, which is itself cut and sent to the laboratories to provide a carefully graded pristine 'show copy', which is what the audience sees in the cinema or on television.

The quality of the UK video was atrocious. For some unknown reason scenes were excised from the original and the sound track is out of synchronisation. It's a disgrace and an insult to all who worked on it to have it on public sale.

When first I viewed a copy in 1994, I tried, without success, to have it withdrawn from sale. The company that released it deservedly went into liquidation and the people who subsequently acquired the 'Special' changed the title and only gave it a limited release.

What this appalling video does, however, is give a clear idea of the script quality. Admittedly, ours were not up to Galton and Simpson standards, but they weren't very far off, and they were certainly better than any Tony had after he abandoned the BBC.

Years later, Hugh Stuckey met Galton and Simpson. 'They said something very revealing to me,' remembers Hugh. 'They said, "We saw all your scripts. They were good. But," they said, "you wrote for the Tony Hancock we wrote for, but by the time he got to you, he wasn't that Tony any more." And it's true, because I wrote knowing Hancock from what I'd seen on television.' I mentioned this to Philip Oakes, who observed: 'I think he'd drunk several vats of hard stuff before he got to you.'

Had Tony been in good form and delivered something approaching his *Hancock's Half-Hour* standard of excellence, those scripts would have been highly acclaimed.

I have no doubt that the series premise itself was bang on target. The lad from East Cheam migrates to the 'Colonies', where he expects to discover an antipodean Utopia. But instead of leaving his Hancockian prejudices behind, he drags them to the other side of the globe, where he dismally fails to come to terms with the Australian life style. And vice versa!

We tried to distill the essence of the series into Ron Jubb's splendid 60-second opening animated cartoon title sequence. After a pretentious fanfare accompanying the circular Channel Seven logo zooming back into the compass drawing in the corner of a mock antique map of the world, we hear 'Rule Britannia' as the camera closes in on England. The picture dissolves to a tricorn-hatted Captain James Cook as his eighteenth-century sailing ship rides a wave twice its height while a plummy, portentous English public school voice declares, 'Two hundred years ago, James Cook set forth from England to seek an enticing new land called Terra Australis upon which to plant *The* Flag.'

On the words '*The* Flag', the camera zooms past Captain Cook raising a telescope to his eye, into a full-screen shot of the Union Jack and the music segues into the specially composed series theme – loosely based on the original Hancock tuba theme – 'Pada da dum pum pum'.

A dissolve from the flag reveals an ocean liner about to set sail from southern England as the voice intones, 'To emulate the traditions set by the early empire builders intrepid Englishmen follow to the antipodean colony to this very day.'

The liner starts to pull away, but remains tethered to England. It rears back, attempting to break the rope, but the rope holds and the liner's effort separates England from Scotland and away the liner sails with England in tow. The ship sails down the curvature of the earth, the Union Jack fluttering proudly behind it.

Cut to a Homburg-hatted, astrakhan-coated cartoon Hancock who turns his binoculars to camera on the words 'intrepid Englishmen'. His eyes, enlarged by the binocular lenses, blink at

85

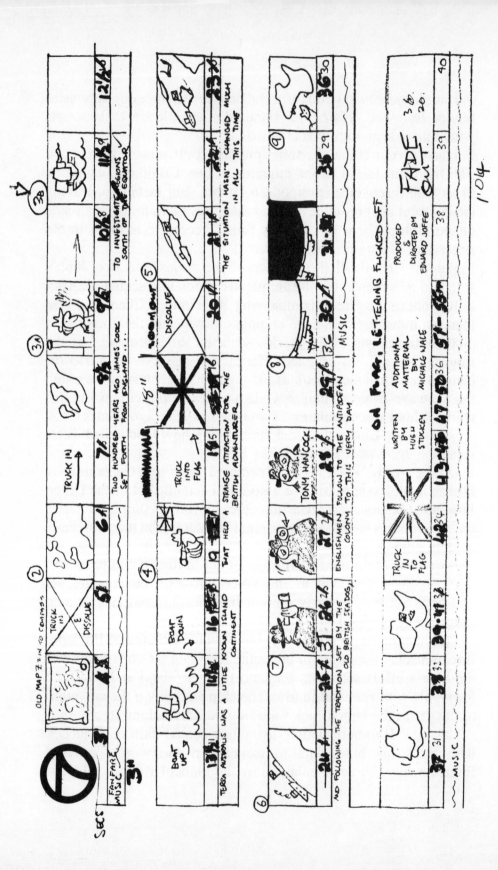

the audience. The word *Hancock* is superimposed below the binoculars.

In the next picture the liner sails upside down, still tugging England and its Union flag towards Terra Australis. It steams into the Great Australian Bight which turns into a shark's jaws which bite (geddit), chew and swallow both the liner and England. The shark reverts to the shape of Australia, which burps and regurgitates the Homburg hat and the flag. The camera zooms into a full-screen shot of the flag on which other credits are superimposed.

The music, the voice and the words were exactly right. It's not only great fun, but it perfectly captured the theme. Tony loved the idea but never saw the finished product.

There had been much discussion about a series title. At one stage *Pommie's Progress* seemed a possibility, but this was soon changed to *Hancock Down Under*, which we definitely couldn't use after Tony's death, so by common consent it was agreed that the only appropriate title would simply be *Hancock*.

The series' comic potential was enormous, having as it did, a selection of well conceived, interesting supporting characters, including a one-sided love interest in the shape of a buxom, blonde, randy, widowed landlady, whose ambition it is to get Tony into the sack. He can't stand her. Everything she does is way over the top, her personality, her awful, ersatz 1960s furnishings, Tretchikoff's *Chinese Lady*, a set of flying ducks frozen on the hideous wallpaper, seashell ornaments and so on. Her bedroom was a masterpiece of bad taste, with large open Spanish fans, swag drapes, red flocked wallpaper, brass bedstead and a Dolly Varden kidney-shaped dressing table.

The art director admirably captured the ambience of the worst possible taste of the era (or any other era, for that matter). It was a sort of Hancock meets *Neighbours* as they might have been in the Swingin' Sixties . . . Imagine Hancock in *Neighbours*. That's what we tried to do some 20 years before *Neighbours* was dreamt up.

12

'Come in, Little Tich'

A glum cloud hung over the meeting I had with Jim Oswin and Geoff Healy. Healy had briefed Oswin about the studio disaster, but Oswin wanted to hear it directly from my lips. After I told him what had happened he invited my suggestions as to what we should do. My answer was that there was only one thing to do. Pack it in and save a lot of money. Silence. Oswin was reluctant to abandon the project. Did I have any ideas on how to proceed? I said Tony was incapable of completing the series as he was unlikely to give up drinking.

Our shooting ratio on the pilot had been enormous. The shooting ratio is the overall number of times sequences are filmed in relation to the total number of feet shot throughout the production. If it were possible to limit each take to one, the shooting ratio would be 1:1, two cracks at it would be 2:1 et cetera. Using the multicamera system, my anticipated shooting ratio was four to one. Maximum. The average for a fairly straightforward production without complex effects, chases, far-flung locations, minimal technical hitches and shot on a single camera using film techniques would be about 10:1. The dozens of retakes on the pilot took our ratio to about 15:1.

My thoughtfulness in wanting to save ATN-7 many hundreds of Australian dollars by not processing the film shot on the second day was appreciated by the executives, who favoured processing and editing several scenes in order to give the Board a clearer idea of content before making any judgments or decisions.

I left them to consider the situation. The outcome was that they processed the lot and a few sequences were hurriedly cobbled together. I was not invited to the executive screening.

My team spent that week in limbo. The ball was firmly in the management court, and all we could do was wait to see what they chose to do.

Tony was on tenterhooks and telephoned me constantly to ask if I'd seen the rushes yet and when would we complete the episode? I couldn't bring myself to tell him that I was sure the series would be abandoned, so I made excuses about technical problems at the laboratories. I doubt he believed me, but I assured him that he would be the second person to know the moment I was informed. I hated myself for the lie, but had I divulged my thoughts, it would have provided Tony with a reason – as if one were needed – to hit the sauce even harder than usual.

The Australian management weren't stalling intentionally. They really didn't know what to do.

Jim Oswin consulted the Chairman, and so serious was the situation that the Chairman in turn consulted his board. At my next meeting with Jim Oswin I was asked if it would be feasible to replace Tony. As the scripts had been written in Hancockian style specifically for Tony, I argued that substantial rewriting would be necessary to make them work for someone else. Nevertheless I was asked to recommend potential replacements.

It was obvious that Harry H. Corbett from *Steptoe and Son* was by far the best choice. In my opinion he was the only choice, and his agent was contacted but he passed.

A fortune had already been lavished on the series and the Australians didn't want it all flushed down the pan, so Franz Conde began a telephone marathon to London agents to try to find a replacement. Ideally they wanted an actor who would be known to Australian viewers, but the list wasn't that extensive. On my recommendation Phyllis Rounce was again enlisted, and she called many of her contacts, to no avail. Lesser lights were approached, but there were no takers. Anything associated with Hancock, it seemed, was baaaad news.

As I had no idea of what might happen with the series, I was unable to pass any information to my production team. I would have wagered that the series would be ditched, and no one on the team seriously expected anything other than that. There really wasn't much anyone could do except hang about and speculate.

At this stage negotiations for my producer/director contract hadn't been finalised. I was worried about finances because Collins, who had concocted my contract in the first place for ATN-7, had inserted a clause stipulating a lower rate during pre-production weeks than I was to receive in a production (i.e. shooting) week. I'd never heard of a deal like this before. Generally directors receive either an all-in fee for a series or are paid for every working week, regardless of whether the series is in pre-production, production or post-production. However, Collins hadn't reckoned on fallow weeks, and I could see a lot of those coming up. Jack Neary felt that this oversight would ensure that I was paid at least the same weekly fee as the agreed pre-production rate. So the telephoning and telexing and cabling ring-a-roses between myself, Jack Neary, Hugh Alexander at International Artists in London and ATN-7 was renewed. Obviously ATN-7 could not have foreseen what happened and they baulked at having to pay me for not working so they stopped payments, pending legal advice!

Although money had not been the major inducement in my decision to go to Australia to work with Tony, I had my family and mortgage to maintain in the UK and it was essential for me to receive a regular income.

The management's attitude didn't exactly endear them to me, and I was forced to turn to my father-in-law for a loan to meet my UK commitments.

There was a whole lot of doom and gloom going on while we waited for decisions, so the writers and I decided to treat Tony to lunch to boost his morale. And ours. He persuaded us to dine at his hotel, where the food was commendable and we sank a great deal of fine Australian vintage wine. Tony wasn't a frequent visitor to the restaurant there and his appearance was, for the staff, an event, and we enjoyed the best service imaginable at a quiet, secluded table. Away from the gawpers Tony hated so much, the Hancock charm was bright as a beacon that day and the staff were ecstatic at having him there.

During dessert, the manager came over to enquire if everything was satisfactory and invited us to have a brandy on the house. We thanked him for his offer, and he returned a few minutes later wearing a large smile and bearing a bottle of hundred-year-old Cognac. He poured us all a double and Tony invited him to join us, which he did. He told us that the hotel group had bought a case of the Cognac at auction and had limited their hotels to one bottle each, to be reserved for very special VIPs and, it seemed, Tony was it. The bar price for that brandy was 25 Australian dollars a tot! We finished the entire bottle and the manager refused to let us pay anything towards it! The plan had been for us to buy Tony lunch, but he would have none of it and signed for the meal. We all left the restaurant in high spirits and not a penny poorer, since ATN-7 were still footing Tony's hotel bills.

We adjourned to Tony's room where we swapped anecdotes. Tony hated jokes. He loved anecdotes and was a brilliant, but brilliant, raconteur who kept us absorbed for hours. Tony was too hot so he took a shower, emerging wrapped in a towel. He began a story which, he said, he'd acquired direct from Laurence Olivier, and he told it in a superb imitation of Olivier's voice and mannerisms. The story concerned a very small music hall artiste called Little Tich, with whom Olivier had once worked. Little Tich, whose reputation was legendary, so we were informed, was under four-foot six-inches tall. Olivier told Tony that he, Larry, was going to leave the room and once outside, he was going to knock on the door. Tony was to ask, 'Who's there?' to which Olivier said he would reply, 'Little Tich.' Olivier instructed Tony to respond by saying, 'Come in, Little Tich.'

'Got that?' Tony asked us.

'Yes,' we all replied.

'Right,' said Tony, in his own voice, 'I'm Olivier. I'm going outside and I'm going to knock on the door and you're all to say, "Who's there?" I'll say, "Little Tich", and you're to say, "Come in, Little Tich." Got that?'

'Yes,' we said.

Up he rose from the bed on which he lay, and off fell the towel. Unaware that he'd lost it, Tony opened the door to the outside corridor.

'You can't go out like that, Tony,' someone said, 'people pass by all the time – you'll get had up!'

Tony picked up the towel and started tucking it round his waist as he left.

'Just remember your lines,' he retorted, and out he went, closing the door behind him. Almost immediately there was a knock on the door.

'Who's there?' we chorused.

Back came Olivier's voice, 'Little Tich.'

'Come in, Little Tich,' we chanted in unison.

The door opened.

Our eyes naturally focused at Tony's height, about the five-foot-ten level, but at first glance there was no one there, until we looked down and saw a person about four-foot-six high. Tony was on his knees, and, having again lost the towel, he was naked as the day he was born, hurrying in, walking on his knees. He was Little Tich.

13

'I'm going to take the cure'

Insecurity built up enormous tension and with it Tony's bombardment of telephone calls to me at all hours continued unabated.

'It's typical,' he complained, 'it's typical of these colonials to bugger us about. Why don't we take it all back to England and shoot it there?' Even so, he forced a smile from me: 'The only fucking thing they're any good at here is cricket,' he declared before he hung up.

No one had the courage to tell him quite how appalling the pilot had been. In spite of his Hancockian bravado, he must have known it was all over, and his last vestige of self-respect was rapidly dwindling. He seemed to hope that some miracle would occur, that somehow it would be all right on the night. But I'm afraid it wasn't.

'So what happens next?' Was Clare's rhetorical question to her parents. 'There will be meetings now to decide whether or not we try to continue the series, or set up something else to do in the colour studio.

'...which brings me,' she continued, 'to ATN-7, the station which currently pays me to sit on my backside or indeed lie on the beach in the Autumn sun ... There is talk of drying out poor Hancock and doing the series with him but if I'm any judge, it's far too late and anyway doesn't it take ages to dry someone out?'

ATN-7 remained in a quandary. Abandon the series? Cut losses? Find a new lead? What do we do?

The press speculated. Rumours were rife. Tony was going through a living death of suspense and I just couldn't bring myself to spell out to him what everybody knew. He was obsessed about flying back to England, continually proclaiming, 'We could do the damn thing properly over there.' He insisted his UK contacts would finance the project, but I knew this was a forlorn hope.

On the morning of Monday 29 April Jim Oswin told me the Chairman wanted to see me immediately. Mr Rupert Henderson, Chairman of the board of ATN-7, which also owned a number of newspapers and, it seemed, half of Sydney, had never been seen before by anyone on our production team let alone met him, and I wasn't sure what to expect. I had a feeling that Mr Big would be a strapping, dynamic Australian in the Kerry Packer mould. I found a clone of a very different kind.

Mr Henderson was a wee, sparrow-like man with a desk the size of a billiard table. He wore a shirt that was an inch too large for him, and apart from his teeth, his expensive clothes, a decent shave and haircut, he was a ringer for Wilfred Brambell, Harold Steptoe's father in *Steptoe and Son*.

I had expected him to be surrounded by a coterie of advisers, accountants, executives and what have you, but he was alone. I sensed that his office was the place where the buck stopped.

He courteously shook my hand, thanked me for coming and got straight to business without any small talk.

'Well,' he said, 'what are we going to do?'

I repeated what I'd told Jim Oswin. 'There's only one thing you can do,' I replied, 'abandon the series and cut your losses.'

The Chairman confirmed my suspicions that that was what he had in mind and he asked if we could get a replacement from England.

He knew that this had been tried, but he wanted to hear it from me, so I obliged and told him that Harry H. Corbett had turned it down. As had many others.

He thanked me for being frank with him, then sat back thoughtfully for a few moments before asking, 'Do you think we could dry him out?'

I expressed my doubts by telling him what I knew he already

94

knew, that Tony had taken 'the cure' many, many times without any lasting success.

He looked me straight in the eye. 'Fire him,' he said dispassionately.

I could not bring myself to wield the executioner's axe. I told the Chairman that Tony and I both worked for him, and that if any firing was to be done, I couldn't do it. Not to Hancock.

'All right,' he said, 'I'll do it. Have him here at noon tomorrow.'

There hadn't been time to tell Tony of my sudden summons to the Chairman's office and I hadn't the balls to talk to him face to face, so I telephoned him. He repeated the usual litany of questions. Had I seen the rushes? What the hell did they think they were doing? Why all the delay? Why don't we go back to England?

I was too depressed to flannel him with the usual answers and excuses, but I had somehow to prepare him for the inevitable.

'I've seen the Chairman, Tony. He wants to speak to you personally.'

'I don't want to speak to him,' he said defensively.

I told Tony that the Chairman seemed to be a reasonable man and that he should talk to him.

'What about? What about?' he demanded to know.

I told him there was a danger of the whole thing being called off unless he saw the Chairman. I said I felt there was only one way we could continue with the production, and that was if he agreed to dry out.

He repeated what he'd told me in the past: 'I can't do it, Ed, I've been through this before. It's agony.'

I could no longer restrain myself. 'Tony,' I said, 'this is your last chance.' I spoke slowly, as if trying to underline each word so that it would penetrate whatever part of his brain it needed to reach.

He tried to change the subject, yet again reciting the 'Let's take the whole thing to England' bit. Somehow Tony believed this was an option.

I cut him short. The time for evading the issue was over.

Stronger language was called for. 'Tony,' I said, 'if you don't do it, the series is over... If you fuck up in Australia, there's nowhere else to go.'

Dusty Nelson delivered Tony to the Chairman next day at noon. Tony promised to telephone me as soon as the meeting ended. A very long three hours after his appointment, my phone jangled. I picked it up on the first ring.

'Ed,' he said, 'I've decided.' There was a long pause. His motto was 'Make 'em laugh, make 'em cry, but above all, make 'em wait'. Nothing impaired the timing of his next line – at that moment I was on the edge of my seat. 'Ed,' another agonising pause, 'I'm going to take the cure.' I wept. With joy.

'Where are you?' I asked.

He was at Cavell House Private Hospital at Rose Bay. I went straight round to see him. Dusty had dropped him there and left after Tony had signed in.

I never found out precisely what was discussed between Tony and Henderson at that meeting. It had lasted over an hour (mine had taken less than ten minutes), but my guess is that despite all the wasted money and effort, the Chairman must have taken a shine to him. Tony did not volunteer to take the cure, he'd been ordered to do it in terms Tony understood and respected. The Chairman said, 'I want you to take the cure now. Today. Immediately. One more drink, mate, and you're on the first bloody plane back to Blighty.'

Henderson picked up his phone. Tony was admitted to the clinic an hour later.

When I got there, Tony was sitting up in bed in a dressing gown. He seemed quite chirpy because the waiting game was over for him and he could now relax, for a while anyway, until the treatment began in earnest.

Henderson agreed that the station would foot all the bills and do everything necessary to get Tony back to normal. Few people would have taken so calculated a risk, but Henderson did, and he deserves praise for his compassion. That meeting extended Tony's life – for at least eight weeks anyway.

The odds were long. Tony had been thrown a life belt and was now in the lifeboat, but the storm within him raged on. He'd been given a chance in a million, and he began the greatest battle of his life.

The nurses at the hospital told me how, when treating alcoholics, the game plan is to gradually reduce the daily intake until it dwindles to the stage where all the patient is left with is a sniff. Thus patients are weaned off alcohol over a period of time. Tony demanded cold turkey – the immediate and complete cessation of alcohol intake. He would argue with the nurse proffering his tapering-off tots. Fortunately his nurses were used to dealing with difficult patients and refused to be intimidated by Tony's gruffness. He put each of them through a regular charade of his refusing and her cajoling him to down his ration, which he'd eventually knock back in one gulp as if it were some bitter medicine. I only witnessed this tragi-comedy once and hoped that perhaps one day we might base a scene on this performance in a *Blood Donor*-type show about an alcoholic.

When he was admitted to the clinic he'd shown a brave face and the sort of braggadocio displayed by his TV persona. He was the cocky Blood Donor incarnate. The next day, however, this had begun to wear off and he sat up in bed, scowling at the world, dressed in ghastly hospital issue pyjamas. I offered to collect his pyjamas from the hotel, but as he didn't own any, I said I'd buy him a few pairs. He insisted they should be plain as he considered that striped pyjamas made him look ridiculous.

It wasn't long before the shakes began in earnest. These were the DTs, and although I'd heard about delirium tremens and seen them portrayed in movies, I'd never before witnessed them live. Tony was enduring the hell he had previously and lucidly described to me. But how he fought!

It was pitiful watching him willing his trembling hands to stir his coffee or struggling to lift to his lips a cup rattling against its saucer, scorning help from me or the duty nurse. The drugs and the withdrawal symptoms took a great deal out of him physically, and he grew weaker and more listless day by day.

Neither of us could be described as masters, but we both played a little chess. Tony loved the game and had presented me with a set. I took it to the hospital to help him while away the long hours. We'd had several games before, and even when tipsy he'd easily beaten me, but his concentration was at such a low ebb in hospital that I could have had a first win in a few moves, but didn't. He twigged what I was up to and greatly resented my patronising him this way.

Tony wanted me to talk about anything. Everything. I did, except for the series we were working on. I told him about my childhood and school days, and the escapades of some of my more eccentric friends seemed to amuse him, particularly those of one Jack Sholomir, who had stowed away in my cabin on a Union Castle ship en route to Southampton from Cape Town, and when I persuaded him to give himself up, had two ocean liners heave to in mid-Atlantic. He was rowed across in the custody of the Master-at-Arms and put on board the ship sailing south. The same guy then walked, yes walked, from South Africa to England. It only took him two years, and he wrote a book about his adventures prior to his becoming a fire eater. Tony approved of that.

We discussed literature. Tony particularly admired Leonard Cottrell's work. He hadn't got round to *The Tiger of Ch'in*, which I bought and read aloud to him. He enjoyed this and struggled to remain awake long enough to hear how things panned out. I still treasure two of Tony's Cottrell books – *Queen of the Pharaohs* and *The Land of Shinar*.

When he was in the mood for conversation he'd tend to doze off in mid-sentence.

In the Sixties television sets in hospitals were unheard of, but with his doctors' approval I borrowed a small portable from the studio for his use. He slept through much of the local programming, regarding it as a cure for insomnia, and confided that he intended to retire on the fortune he would make from importing the shows to England for that purpose.

The press were baying at our heels like hungry dingoes, desperate to dine on Tony's distress. They wanted to know where Tony was, why, and for how long. It is fairly certain that they knew what had happened. There had been too many people in the studio for word of the disastrous pilot not to have leaked out, but apart from myself and a handful of senior ATN-7 management, only Clare, Dusty, Hugh and Mike were entrusted with knowledge of his whereabouts. ATN-7 didn't want to risk a major scandal.

We liaised as far as possible to visit him in shifts, because he couldn't cope with lots of people and was much happier when he saw us individually. Hugh Stuckey's home was in Melbourne and he returned there to be with his family, telephoning in daily to check on how Tony was faring.

Because of Tony's incarceration, I was able to involve myself directly in my contract negotiations. I was also investigating the possibility of making a documentary film for ATN-7 and couldn't spend as much time with Tony as I would have wished.

Nevertheless I saw him every day, sometimes twice a day. It was like watching a boxing match in instalments, with a former champ being knocked down regularly, but stubbornly rising again, punch drunk, only to absorb more and increasingly powerful blows.

His production team and all the staff at the hospital were rooting for him and his almost superhuman efforts to overcome his opponent.

When his shakes were at their worst, he was heavily sedated, but somehow he mustered hidden reserves of strength to make extensive, expensive telephone calls to England to talk to his mother, to his solicitors and trying, unsuccessfully, to reach his mistress. He kept asking for Clare to visit him and he would talk to her about Joan.

I knew nothing about Joan at the time except her first name. That Tony was madly, boyishly, in love with her is beyond question. He lived for her letters. His face lit up when he received her letters. He kept and treasured them and enjoyed reading excerpts from them aloud to me when we were alone. They were very moving in parts, and Joan obviously reciprocated his feelings.

Like a lovesick schoolboy, he would gush over the fact that she had emulsioned a dresser, making it sound as if she'd just painted the ceiling of the Sistine Chapel.

An intimate friend of Tony's confided in me that Cicely had

99

become pregnant at a time when they were short of money and they decided on an abortion. Something went wrong, and Cicely was rendered barren. During his *Face to Face* interview, John Freeman asked him if he'd like to have children. Tony was emphatic, uncompromising. 'No,' he answered unequivocally. Tony was forever changing his mind, and if he was still with Cicely when he eventually decided he wanted to be a father after all, the fact that she couldn't oblige may have contributed to the breakdown of their marriage.

'If I was two days late or whatever,' Joan Le Mesurier told me, 'he'd phone up his mum and say, "I think she's pregnant. I think we've done it this time." If we made love he'd say, "I just know that was the one." We tried a lot.'

'Why,' I wondered, 'did he want a baby so badly?'

'It would have been a way of securing our relationship,' said Joan, 'he was very insecure. I'd said to Tony, "If you can stay off the booze for a year – if you can prove you can do this for a year, I will leave John and I'll marry you."'

John Le Mesurier was aware of the affair – and had been from the time it began – but, impeccable English gentleman that he was, he had resigned himself to the inevitable.

Joan lived with Tony for about a year. Their fights replicated those he had with Cicely and Freddie. The last straw for Joan was when Tony came home after a lost weekend lasting five days.

Joan recalls: 'When he turned up with his tie round the back of his neck – the knot at the back of his head; his trousers were sort of hanging over his hips, they were always slipping down – I opened the door to this wreck – this unshaven, stinking wreck and I said, "Where have you been?" And he said, "You would have been proud of me, I've been helping a sick friend out."'

He'd spent the time with Cicely.

'He was very fond of Cicely,' Joan told me, 'she was an accomplice in crime. She had the same problem as him, and when he went off on that last jaunt, which broke us up from living together, it was with her. He went and got pissed with her. Those five days, he was with her. Of course he left her in a right state, I should imagine.'

Joan returned to John Le Mesurier. It was November 1967, only a few months before Tony left for Australia. But it wasn't over between them, and by December they were back together again.

In his book *A Jobbing Actor*, John wrote: 'I did not then know – or perhaps did not want to know – about Joan's continuing relationship with Tony. I behaved tolerably well.' An understatement of vast proportions. John loved Joan deeply. Joan loved John. And Tony. And Tony loved them both.

Joan's clandestine double life presented her with logistical problems. 'I was back with John,' she told me, 'and I was sneaking around to Tony every day when John was at work and looking after Tony then running back to John. It was just a nightmare.'

The affair was further complicated by her parents' disapproval and another woman – a fine character actress, Damaris Hayman – with whom Tony had a platonic relationship. When Tony first told Joan he'd taken a woman to Bournemouth to visit his mother, Joan admits pangs of jealousy at first, but his friendship with Damaris helped Joan's peace of mind. 'It was a relief,' Joan wrote, 'to know that he wasn't alone at night half-drugged and falling about or drunk and depressed.'

Damaris Hayman, who considers herself 'A rather upper-crust character lady who has worked with everybody from Hancock down', told me: 'I was very fond of him and, if he rang me, whatever time it was, including the middle of the night, I would go round there and talk to him and we would play records and I would make him endless cups of rather nasty tea. I used to read aloud to him because he'd had a bang on the head and thought he was going blind, which he wasn't, but wouldn't go to an oculist and get some reading glasses. And he liked the way I read aloud, so I read aloud. It was anything from Winnie the Pooh to Plato,' she said, 'I was there a lot but I wasn't his mistress.'

Joan had no doubts whatever about Tony's love for her. 'He was very passionately in love with me,' she said. Tony's letters to Joan were, in her words: 'Quite childish and rather soppy and

101

romantic. They were, well, loving. Not sexy, not a bit sexy, he didn't write rude things ... just how much he loved me – very tender and always imploring – "please don't let this end..."'

Joan has been most gracious to permit me to publish, for the first time, a few excerpts from those cherished letters.

Tony's letter to her en route to Australia, dated 8 March 1968, said: 'My darling – I'm already missing you so badly...'

'I love the way you describe things,' he wrote later, 'and I know how repetitive one feels as you try to show all your love and affection on paper. Nevertheless I do love you completely and shall repeat it again and again and expect you to do the same.'

Another letter: 'I will write again as soon as I possibly can. You are never out of my mind. With all my love always. Tony.'

And the next: 'No letter came today or yesterday so naturally I was a bit disappointed so no doubt you have problems to be on your own. My love to everybody who is approachable and of course to you. The more I hear from you, the more it helps. My love always. Tony.'

Yet another: 'I love you more every day and long for the time when we can be with each other quite openly.'

No one except Joan knew of Tony's secret agenda. 'As I probably mentioned,' he wrote, 'I intend to split the series up into three parts so I can come home for a while. It has been unbearable sometimes without you and only by concentrating on the work can I vaguely put you out of my mind.'

The fate of the series remained in limbo. It was pointless to even think about plans, either personal or professional, until such time as we knew that the pivotal figure would be able to tackle the immense task that lay before him. With Tony in hospital, neither the production team nor the management knew how to handle the situation.

There were simply too many unanswered questions. Do we plan ahead with scripts, sets, cast and so on and if so, what is it going to cost, and what if Tony doesn't make it, and if he does will he be able to work, and if so, when? It was a very trying time – not just for Tony...

A few days after Tony's hospitalisation Clare wrote: 'It's Monday morning now and I'm just off to my mad job. Hancock is having DTs in a clinic, and we are having them at Channel 7.'

Of course no one knew how long it would take to 'cure' Tony, and most freelance members of my production team were laid off and our ATN-7 staff crew redeployed to other shows.

I resolved my own financial problem and ensured regular weekly payment by persuading management to let me make a documentary for them about King's Cross, the vibrant low-life, nightlife district of Sydney.

This gave the ATN-7 management a face-saving opportunity to hedge their bets by continuing to pay me since I was now gainfully employed by them. If they had terminated my contract, as they did with others on our team, I would have had to return to the UK immediately, which would have presented them with the problem of replacing me as, when and *if* Tony recovered. During the discussions about my new contract, I discovered that I was receiving substantially less than Collins had budgeted for.

Tony knew King's Cross and loved its atmosphere, variously described as dazzling, glittering, sparkling, fabulous, colourful and so on. . . . It could also be defined as tacky, corrupt, wicked and dangerous, depending on the angle you viewed it from.

When Sydney folk wanted a sleazy, boozy night out, they'd generally spend it 'Up at the Cross', and that's what I decided to call the film. King's Cross at that time was a steamy, dangerous place, peopled as it was, by whores of both sexes, strippers ditto, pimps, transvestites, drag queens, gays, lesbians, con men, muggers, and tourists. There were naturally a lot of ordinary residents, but they were hard to spot.

Tony was quite excited with my plans and made me promise to let him voice the commentary.

Researching this film left me even less time to visit Tony, but it kept me busy and provided lots of anecdotes about our filming sessions.

Tony was intrigued by the adventures my small film unit encountered while working, and he chuckled away at incidents, particularly the more risqué ones concerning the female impersonators

103

who were almost as notorious as the area itself. Les Girls was the best-known showcase.

The Les Girls productions aspired to emulate those of Las Vegas, but they didn't make it quite so spectacularly with only 15 'girls', a lot less talent and a very restricted budget. The owner agreed to allow filming on their quietest night, and I reached the venue an hour or so before the crew to organise the shoot and to get to know who was who.

I knocked on the dressing room door. A voice invited me in and there, in front of the large mirrors with their bare light bulbs, sat a glorious creature, naked from the waist up, with breasts to rival any centrefold girl. When I got my breath back, I apologised and said, 'Sorry, I thought this was the boys' dressing room.' 'It's OK,' was the husky reply, 'it is.' I realised I'd lead a very sheltered life.

Only one or two of the artistes hadn't yet had silicone implants. Some of them were saving up to go to Japan for 'The Operation' to transform them into women. It was hard to believe that they were all men, the only giveaway being their hands and waists. One tawny-haired six-footer who basked in the name of Carlotta, wanted to know if I was married. I asked why s/he asked, and was told: ''Cos I fancy you.'

'I fancy you too,' I said, 'but what am I going to do with you?'

The other girls roared with laughter, as did Tony when I told him about it.

Statuesque Carlotta was not only the star of the show, she had become the talk of the town courtesy of a touring UK rugby team. When they visited the club one of the players invited Carlotta to join him at his table. They got on famously and subsequently dated.

The smitten rugby player proposed and was accepted. Apparently he'd failed to spot the three doors to the toilets were marked 'His', 'Hers' and '???'. Or, if he had, the penny didn't drop. Naturally, in the true spirit of rugby humour, his team-mates kept shtum about it until the eve of their departure from Sydney, by which time the poor sod had bought an expensive ring... When they told him, he went berserk and rushed off to Les Girls. Fortunately for Carlotta, he was arrested before Carlotta reached the club, and the 'rugger bugger' – Tony's term – only had to pay for destroying furniture instead of being charged with GBH or attempted murder.

One Saturday night, the busiest night of the week for the staff, we were filming in the casualty department of the hospital in King's Cross. There was nothing special happening, a doctor assured me as he tended a guy whose ear had been bitten off, 'Just an average Saturday night out, with people having a good time.' He then moved on to the queue of bloody noses, gashed heads, broken teeth and black eyes.

This was the hospital where most of the 'girls' came for regular check-ups. In between their tender ministrations to damaged revellers, the nurses told us that whenever a new houseman reported for duty they made sure that the first 'girl' to check in was examined by him. In nine cases out of ten, the aspiring doctor never spotted the difference.

On another evening, we were preparing to shoot a fire engine emerging from the local fire station when three young women stopped to ask what we were up to. I thought they were prostitutes and asked if we could interview them. They told me they weren't what I thought they were, and I immediately realised that they too, were transsexuals, so I said: 'That's OK, we'd still like to film you.'

While the crew unloaded the equipment and set up to film outside a men's outfitting shop, I took the 'girls' into a café for coffee and to work out what questions they would be prepared to answer.

King's Cross had made Sydney a favourite city for US servicemen fighting the Vietnam war to spend their R and R (Rest and Rehabilitation leave). They chose Australia, I was told, in preference to Japan, because the Australians spoke English. Tony smiled when I told him that. 'We know better, don't we?' he said.

The three 'girls', who were also saving up for The Operation, owed their livelihood to the Yanks. They assured me that their clients never discovered their secret and they elaborated on their professional activities and how they did what and to whom.

I paid full attention to the details of their modus operandi, wanting to remember every word for Tony's benefit. My glazed concentration must have been mistaken for boredom because one of them snapped at me, saying s/he didn't think I believed what s/he was telling me, which was that s/he had real breasts. Remembering Les Girls, I assured him/her that I was a believer, but by then s/he had started unbuttoning his/her blouse. Talk about timing, the waiter with our coffees arrived at the very instant a plump breast hove into view.

The waiter executed the most perfect double take I have ever seen. His mouth opened very wide, and I thought his eyes were going to pop out.

'See,' proclaimed the proud owner, 'it's real.' Just as the second piece of evidence was released, the Italian proprietor of the café stormed across and ordered us out: 'I don' wanna girlsa likea you inna my place. Geddout!'

The 'girls' regarded this as a compliment to their femininity and found it very droll. So did Tony.

Tony also relished the story of our attempt to film in the gay bar in an hotel near the El Alamein memorial fountain in King's Cross. Australian humour is not dissimilar to that of rugby players, and being both, the manager approved our filming with a wry smile, deciding to let us discover for ourselves what he damn well knew was going to happen.

The gay guys weren't in the least interested in starring in my film, and the crew were unceremoniously frogmarched out by some massive cobbers who would not have been out of place in a Mr America contest.

Then they spotted us trying to photograph them on the pavement from inside the camera van, and they taught us the real meaning of rock'n'roll by physically rocking the van so violently that it almost capsized before the terrified driver managed to start it and sped away in a cloud of burning rubber.

This event certainly changed my mind about some covert filming of the whorehouses known locally as Borg houses. These old houses, originally built for single bachelors, were tiny, one-roomed brothels. It seems the legal definition of a brothel was a house with 'more than one' woman. Thus a single tart in a house

106

didn't constitute a brothel, and a certain gentleman called Borg had exploited this loophole by buying up rows of these little buildings which were tailor-made for one-woman operations. Apparently the police were powerless to do anything about them. One dark night, Borg's car exploded with him in it, and no one knew, or dared grass on the perpetrator. Tony decided it must have been the cops.

Tony had won the Battle of Cavell House but did not emerge from the ordeal looking much like a laurelled victor.

He'd lost weight and his clothes were all too big for him, making him look more hunched than ever before. He seemed much greyer than before his incarceration. He was wan, tired, forlorn and bored out of his biscuit. He was chainsmoking. He looked 60 years old. He had spent his 44th birthday in the hospital.

14

'He is infinitely better for the moment'

On the day Tony was admitted to hospital, I asked the distinguished consultant for his prognosis on how long Tony might have to stay there. He refused to even hazard a guess other than it might be three weeks, three months, or more. A measure of Tony's determination to conquer his addiction is manifested by the fact that he left the clinic a mere three weeks later.

The battle was won, but regrettably the war wasn't over.

The ATN-7 executives were not a little relieved. They were delighted that Tony had done so well and that it had been so swift a 'cure'. They took a positive, optimistic view.

After his discharge from hospital, I again asked the consultant how long Tony might stay dry. The eminent expert declined to answer except in the vaguest terms, sticking almost verbatim to his previous script: 'Three weeks?', he said, 'three months maybe, perhaps even as long as six months...'

Under no circumstances, the doctors decreed, was Tony to live alone. Without a family environment they held out no hope whatever of Tony's maintaining his precarious balance on a very rickety wagon. But nobody was prepared to shoulder such a burden. The ATN-7 management somehow persuaded the company doctor, in whom Tony had found a kindred spirit, to take Tony in as a lodger on a temporary basis to allow time to find him a more suitable permanent abode.

Tony's messy life was becoming ever more shambolic and he was beset with problems. The worst, he told me, was that Joan had been instructed by a solicitor not to have any contact with him until after his divorce. The hearing date was approaching rapidly. Tony was telephoning his mother more frequently than ever and writing letters to Joan at a Ramsgate box number.

Due to a postal strike he received no mail from her, and being unable to reach her by phone caused him great distress. He felt Joan had somehow betrayed him, he confided to Clare, alleging that Joan wasn't brave enough to stand by him. He repeatedly told Clare he was going to write to Joan about this. Clare tried her utmost to dissuade him: 'Don't write in bitterness. You can't take back what you've written down on paper,' she remembers saying over and over to him. But her efforts were to no avail and one morning he proclaimed, 'I've written it – I've done it. I've sent that letter.' Clare meant it when she said, 'I wish you hadn't.' Clare had no way of knowing that Joan, well used to these 'final partings', didn't take Tony's letter seriously, especially since it reached her in the same post as an affectionate, loving letter. Neither letter was dated.

The strong possibility of that libel action against him was another burden. In an interview titled 'Hancock Unashamed' in *Chance International*, Tony was quoted as saying, 'The great Delfont Organisation consists entirely of failed performers.'

Towards the end of May 1968 Tony had received correspondence from solicitors stating that his allegations were defamatory to Mr Michael Sullivan of Delfont-Grade and Mr Sydney Grace, a director of the Grade Organisation, and that neither Mr Grace nor Mr Sullivan were failed performers and that Tony's accusation had caused damage to their reputations. The letter required an apology and reserved full rights against Tony.

Tony was deeply upset by this because, he said, he'd enjoyed a long and happy relationship with the Grades and he'd never intended anything harmful. He balefully admitted that the writer, Gareth Powell, had submitted the article to him for clearance before publication, but Tony had not read it thoroughly before approving it.

There is no doubt that he had caused the libel, but, he insisted, if he had said it, the comment had been made flippantly and was probably only intended as a wisecrack. Unfortunately for him, it wasn't a line from a comedy script. In real life and cold print it became another bale of straw on his already heavily overladen back.

Drawing on the luxury of hindsight, so many things seem self-evident, and today I can understand how Tony's problems turned him into a dipsomaniac, and I realise that it was a miracle that he was able to work at all, plagued as he was by such a profusion of the slings and arrows of outrageous fortune.

The Press were still on the prowl. They weren't the only ones interested in Tony's health and the future of the series. The production team depended on these factors for their living.

I eventually received the green light to proceed with six episodes, and production planning began in earnest.

On 12 May Clare wrote: 'The Hancock series is to continue and we are working ourselves silly again. Of course it can't possibly happen really, because the poor man's brain must be permanently damaged and they are allowing him only weeks from now to get better. It's scarcely credible is it?'

I still had another week's filming scheduled on the King's Cross documentary. I thought it would be possible to combine this with my Hancock duties because of the forward planning I had previously completed.

Wrong! Again.

One snag was that certain key members of the team had either been deployed to other projects or had their contracts terminated. Most had found jobs elsewhere, so that in effect we were beginning all over again with several new faces, some of whom Tony didn't take to.

Having had a lot of time to think things over, Tony decided he wanted to play a larger role in pre-production.

To Joan he wrote: 'I have to go to the studio now. I go as often as possible to show that I'm perfectly sober, on the ball and fairly clanking with Antabuse.'

Keen as I was to see him occupied, if only to take his mind off his miseries, I didn't want him concerning himself with minor production matters since he tended to build even molehill difficulties into mountainous problems totally out of proportion to reality.

Tony had once before tried his hand at production during an Independent Television series in England. 'For some reason,' Beryl Vertue remembers, 'he decided he would do everything else, and he became very involved in the costumes and the casting and things he should never have done – that I don't think he knew much about in the first place.'

My concern was that Tony's presence would be seriously counterproductive. He would have been bored to tears at technical meetings with the service departments. Nor was it necessary or desirable for him to attend casting sessions for extras or small walk-on parts. I also feared that our familiarity might start breeding.

It was nevertheless imperative for him to have constant company, and the only person immediately available and willing to look after him was Dusty Nelson. Even before I arrived in Sydney, Dusty and Bob, his father, had entertained Tony. We now relied on Dusty to keep him away from us as much as possible, to keep him happy and, we prayed, to keep him sober...

The number of people assigned to the production team was totally inadequate for a series as ambitious and expensive as this, and we could ill afford to lose Dusty's services, but Tony's sobriety and welfare took precedence over everything else. With Dusty now officially elected Tony's minder, he was naturally unable to make any real contribution to the frenzied efforts needed to reactivate the series. So once again the bulk of the pre-production burden fell on myself and Clare, and this meant abandoning any thought of completing the King's Cross documentary.

The MD was adamant that the budget would not permit any extra staff. He pointed out that other ATN-7 shows employed the same number of people as were allocated to the Hancock series. My contention that our series was far more complex and ambitious than anything previously undertaken by ATN-7, and that Dusty Nelson was too deeply involved in babysitting Tony to provide help with production duties, fell on deaf ears.

111

Tony loved koala bears. Dusty frequently took him to the Sydney Zoo where, despite the wonderful vista of the partly completed Opera House, the bridge, the impressive Sydney business skyline and the boats on the lovely bay, Tony would stare at the koalas for hours on end. Joan Le Mesurier said he had the same affinity for Guy the gorilla at London Zoo. Her explanation was that Tony felt sorry for the wonderful beast sitting there moodily staring into space. 'I know why he felt like that,' she said, 'because he was on show too. People used to do the same to him and he *hated* being stared at – hated it. He said "I'm not a tin of fucking beans, you know!"'

His kinship with koalas was probably stronger than his affection for Guy. You see, someone told him their staple diet of eucalyptus leaves got them stoned. He revelled in this newly acquired nugget of knowledge and several times informed us: 'That's why the poor little buggers hang on to their trees so tightly.' He understood them and identified closely with them.

Much as I needed more hands on deck, I did not envy Dusty, who had his time cut out finding things for Tony to do. After all, you can't keep visiting koala bears every day.

To broaden the series' horizons a number of sequences were due to be shot on location. These were mainly sight gags alleviating the chore Tony underwent trying to learn dialogue. Location work not only allowed us to ease him gently back into the work ethic, it also bought time for building new studio sets, casting small parts, holding production meetings and attending to the myriad pre-production details for the long, hard studio slog which lay ahead.

In the meantime, Tony's recovery enabled my agents to satisfactorily sort out my revised contract, which now included a clause stipulating full payment even during fallow periods.

Rehearsals for Episode One began.

Clare was impressed. 'The Hancock business,' she wrote home, 'is going well now. He is infinitely better for the moment and in script readings last week he was almost on his old form. His Churchillian rendering of the words written inside a British passport had us all rolling on the floor – figuratively speaking of course.'

Personality-wise Tony was brooding and aloof, and between takes he sat quietly on his own and did exactly as directed when he was on camera. But Cavell House had not cured that mean streak...

On 10 June, Clare wrote: 'As I told you, I'm getting very fond of Hancock. He is a most courteous man, and I feel we get on quite well. So, a few weeks ago I invited him to dinner for tonight to see our little house and meet one or two of his fans. Last night – Sunday – I rang to confirm a time and was greeted by a tantrum about a script that had not been rewritten to his liking. Since he was actually with the writers at the time, it did seem a little unreasonable to shout at me. However, I replied soothingly and then asked about tonight. "What time shall I expect you?" I said. "Oh," he said, "we'll have to forget that." It is a great disappointment to the girls who had been thrilled at the thought of meeting him, and we'd all done quite a lot to prepare for the party.'

In his opening scene in the first studio programme, Tony has just come off the loser in the postprandial scramble for deck chairs on the sun deck of the ship. He moves to the rail and muses: 'Look at 'em, rolling about there. A whole nation of sitters – that's what's become of us. It makes you wonder about evolution. If the human body develops those parts that get the most use, well, I'd like to be in England in a couple of hundred years and I'd put most of my money in seat covers.'

Clare's letter describes the behind the scenes build-up to this sequence far more eloquently than I. She wrote: 'There are plenty of bright moments, and there was an incident of particular hilarity on Saturday. One of the scenes is on a liner deck, with Tony standing at the rail (having failed to get a deck chair) complaining about the laziness of the human race and speculating on the likelihood of the part of ourselves that we sit on evolving into our most significant feature (as indeed it is in some cases already!). As he mutters, a large-bottomed lady is supposed to wobble across the deck behind him. A childish gag, I agree, but I didn't write the script. Well, we had asked the booking man to book a lady suitably equipped with a large backside. I was dismayed, therefore, to find the lady in question was a glory to behold, with enormous

113

eyelashes, a mass of auburn hair, a truly magnificent bust and a very small modest rear! "Oh dear," I said, and led her up to the director, who turned her round, looked at the elegant posterior and started roaring for the bookings man. Poor little girl, she was absolutely sweet and said she would wiggle as hard as possible, but it was no good – having seen her panoramic bosom, no one was likely to glance at her behind, and the whole point of the gag was lost. Eddie, the director, meanwhile, had a furious quarrel with the bookings man – all because of a bottom!'

Tony's housing problem had become critical because the ATN-7 doctor had not anticipated that Tony would stay with him for quite so long. In fairness, the doctor had made it quite clear to ATN-7 from the start that Tony's sojourn with him was a short-term measure. Although the station continued to approach people, there were no takers. I was asked if I could recommend anyone.

I was missing my family, and I felt the situation might allow us to be reunited. But I wanted to discuss the pros and cons with Myrtle my (then) wife before mooting the idea to ATN-7.

Our children Lynn, Elaine and Steven were nine, six and three at the time, and my wife had her hands pretty full coping with them on her own without me. She was an adventurous woman, and the idea of babysitting a celebrity was both a challenge and an opportunity to see Australia.

When I told the ATN-7 management that she was prepared to make the journey, they flinched at the costs of flying my family to Sydney and footing the bill for accommodation.

Tony's host, an intelligent and charming man with whom Tony enjoyed lengthy conversations, didn't want a permanent guest and was getting progressively more fed up with the intrusion, and nagged the management unceasingly. This provided the deciding factor. My wife somehow managed to rent our home, pack what she needed, and within seven days she and my kids were winging their way to Oz.

Channel 7 booked us into a plush suite in a swish, modern hotel. Our Sheraton penthouse was the one the Beatles had occupied on their Australian tour. When they heard about this my daughters delightedly played musical beds, alternating each night, evicting

114

their baby brother and their parents to ensure they had both slept in the same bed as Paul McCartney.

My wife's first duty was to find a house to live in as quickly as possible. With a car supplied by Channel 7 and the assistance of some friends, she began her search for a home.

She thought her first choice was ideal, but Tony was too well settled in the womb he'd found in the doctor's 'delightfully dotty' home, as Tony described it to Joan, so with the excuse that the house did not allow him enough privacy, he turned it down. The truth was that he simply didn't want to lose the crutch which the doctor had become, not to mention the risk of noise and the inconvenience of living with young kids he might not like and a woman he didn't know.

My wife takes up the story: 'Literally at a week's notice, we packed our bags and flew out to Sydney. Hancock was not exactly charmed at the idea of having some English woman becoming his chaperone, his guardian or whatever, and we did not exactly get off to a wonderful relationship at the start.

'Eddie was deeply involved in pre-production. Hancock was not actively involved in this, and so we embarked on the task of finding somewhere for all of us to live. When I say "we embarked", I mean the royal "we" which, in this case, was Hancock and I.

'We traipsed through the suburbs of Sydney, looking for some suitable place to afford him some privacy. We looked at one house after another, each of which he deemed totally unsuitable. To say that he was uncooperative would be putting it kindly.

'After seeing about nine or ten places on one particular day, we rolled up at an American plantation-style house that had been occupied by some airline stewardesses. The place was a mess, an absolute mess. I pushed a bedroom door open and could not believe what I saw.

'The room looked like a hurricane had hit it and I said, "What a fucking mess." At which point a deep chortle emanated from behind the door I'd just opened. Tony had wandered off on his own and apparently sought solace in this bedroom, and I didn't know he was there. He chuckled and chuckled and said, "Well,

115

thank God. I thought you were going to be one of these starched, stuck-up fucking British bitches. It's nice to know you're human." '

'And from that time on our relationship changed completely. In fact Hancock and I were thrown together quite a lot, and I got to know him quite well.'

Tony and my wife eventually found a mutually acceptable des.res. – an attractive, double-storeyed house in Birriga Road, Bellevue Hill, a rather salubrious Sydney suburb.

It was unique in that it was wedge-shaped, having to fit, as it did, on the downward slope of quite a steep hill. The main house and entrance was at street level. The floor below had once been connected by an internal staircase which was sealed off when the property was converted for letting purposes. From Tony's point of view the main appeal was that his place was completely self contained, and allowed him family company when he wanted it and privacy when he didn't. Each flat had its own kitchen, bathroom and various other rooms. The top section was much larger and quite elegantly furnished.

In the jargon of the Nineties, Tony's quarters in the smaller apartment would best be defined as minimalist in that it was sparsely furnished. But, as with the top flat, there was a splendid, uninterrupted vista of the city across the Royal Sydney Golf Course.

Not precisely what the doctor had literally ordered, but an arrangement he sanctioned because he wanted shot of his star boarder. Tony was very content with his new abode. It was reported that he'd died in a 'semi-basement', with all the sordid connotations that conjures up. This was simply tabloid sensationalism concocted by one Donald Zec.

My wife remembered: 'We had conversations of a really deep philosophical kind as well as very funny ones. One night he gave me his rendition of Long John Silver, and I laughed 'til the tears ran down my cheeks.

'He talked a lot about his impending divorce, and he seemed sad about the breakdown of this relationship, but he certainly was not suicidal. He was quite pragmatic about it. I think he felt that the breakdown was inevitable. He admitted he wasn't really a good husband, and I got the impression that he had considered Freddie Ross more a mother substitute than a wife.

'We discussed suicide one night, in general terms. It was the same night he did his Long John Silver impression. I can see him right now, standing at this mantelpiece with one leg tucked up behind him, held up by one hand. He leaned against the mantel and pointed his finger at me and said in his Long John voice, "Arrr, Jim lad, them's what threaten never does it!"

'Suicide certainly wasn't anywhere on the horizon, and there was no indication that he might even be thinking of it. His whole demeanour had improved. He was smoking a lot and I don't know what drugs or tranquillisers he had prescribed for him, but he certainly seemed to have settled down quite well.'

15

'There weren't many people who would tangle with me'

Exterior filming started on 25 May.

The first location was simply an establishing shot of Tony entering a huge, modern Rugby League Clubhouse with his milkman, a keep-fit enthusiast who wants to show the Pommie bastard how Australians spend a typical Saturday afternoon. Tony anticipates being taken to a big match of some sort, but the pals always meet in the club bar where, in air-conditioned comfort and the proximity of an inexhaustible supply of beer, they watch the match on television! Naturally the conversation hinges on sport, which presents Tony with the opportunity to boast of his sporting prowess with some lovely lines.

> Sarcastic Aussie: 'Being English,' says he, 'I suppose you'd play more refined sports, like polo.'
> 'I was forced into early retirement,' replies Hancock. 'It was either that or the Tower. He's a poor loser, you know.'

To illustrate the contrast between Tony's yarns and what really happened, we filmed a series of flashbacks. The location was a rugby stadium. Tony reminisces:

> 'There weren't many people who would tangle with me. Ahh, it brings it all back – the roar of the crowd, the sting of the liniment, the nervous tension as you lead the team onto the field.'

Tony, in rugby kit, complete with scrum cap and ball, leads a team on to the pitch where the opposing team are waiting. After much hand shaking, he produces a coin, spins it and looks to see if it's heads or tails. After signalling the teams to change ends, he turns and runs off, waving to a vast cheering crowd.

Back in the studio he flourishes his potter's thumb:

'Of course I would've tossed for England that year if I hadn't dislocated me thumb.'

We had hoped to film at a League Club ground, Rugby League being the hot Australian sport at the time, but not even Tony's popularity would persuade them to allow us to do this just prior to a match. Something, they muttered, about disrupting the TV schedule.

The Rugby Union was far more helpful and even supplied two teams of brawny players for us, and we literally had a cast of thousands of spectators who'd come to see the real match. When Tony ran on and off the field the crowd cheered him enthusiastically. They loved it, we loved it, he loved it and it looked good. Tony was back on form.

Tony's bragging eventually precipitates a fight with one of the milkman's exasperated mates, who tires of the bull this bumptious Pom is throwing at him, with lines like these describing his exploits with The Sport of Kings:

'Ah, Royal Ascot ... The bookies shouting the odds, the ladies in their hats all wishing me bon chance, the dramatic hush as we came under starter's orders...'

The flashback shows various shots of punters and bookies at a racecourse. Tony, in jockey's silks, jodhpurs, cap and all the appurtenances, is on horseback. He enters one of the individual starting stalls. They're off! A man with binoculars follows the horses thundering by. We see Tony in a low-angle medium shot, exhorting his mount onwards by yelling and whipping away furiously. The man with binoculars trains them on the starting gate to reveal Tony, standing horse height, feet astride the sides of the stall, sans horse which has galloped off without him.

> In the bar, Tony tells the lads, 'I thought I might have a go at the Melbourne Cup while I was out here, but for the life of me, I can't find me whip.'

The racecourse scene featured authentic jockeys and real race horses. Tony's mount wasn't so much a Derby winner, more a contender for the Glue Factory Stakes. I was assured that this nag was the oldest racehorse in the country and that Tony would be quite safe on it. After all, we couldn't risk our star on a frisky young racehorse. I never did ask Tony if he'd ever sat on a racehorse before, but he'd had an opportunity to object to our plans at the script conference. He wittered on quite a bit about being adequately insured, but he was determined to prove himself to us and he did all that was asked of him. The problem was getting him into the saddle, and when he eventually managed it he made certain that the wranglers maintained a firm grip on the animal while it was manhandled into its starting stall, due to Tony's inability to get it to move even an inch.

His antics prior to the start of shooting were far funnier than the script, what with him mutely expressing his misgivings by employing most of his extensive repertoire of forlorn faces, and we missed a golden opportunity by not filming the preliminaries. Once aboard he just got on with it, but he was very relieved when he heard me call 'print it' for the last time.

Ludicrous as he'd looked in rugby shorts, Tony was even more bizarre in vivid scarlet and gold jockey's silks, but that outfit wasn't far removed from the man in real life, according to George Fairweather. Tony dropped in to see him one Saturday and suggested a round of golf. George's Club was nearby, but Tony suggested a less popular course, maintaining that George's would be 'too public'.

George wondered what he meant by 'too public'.

'Well, I might be recognised and I don't want people coming up to me while I'm playing,' said Tony, 'I'd rather go out of town a bit, you see.'

George replied: 'Don't be bloody stupid, no one'll bother you on the course.'

'In those days,' George said, 'people wore sort of lovat greys, charcoal greys and black. Now he's just told me he didn't want to be conspicuous, and he arrives at the golf course with a shocking pink pullover, a yellow baseball cap and royal blue trousers. You could see him three bloody holes away, and he'd said he didn't want to be conspicuous! I think he was colour blind for a start.

'He wasn't a bad golfer. I don't think he had a handicap. He didn't go in for competitions and only played now and again. With his money – he was earning big money then – you've never seen such a bag full of rubbish. I told him I had a better set that I bought secondhand to learn on. I said, "With all your money . . ." He said, "Well I don't play a lot." I said, "You can't play at all with these bloody things."'

Mute location work suited Tony. The inserts were purely visual in the best silent comedy tradition. He revelled in them, and although he hadn't fully regained his strength, his performances and inventiveness began to build, rekindling the optimism we'd experienced at that famed first read-through.

Other locations included a Parisian pavement café sequence shot at a place called The Village in King's Cross which had a *très* French look about it. The scenario called for Tony to indulge in some culture and he starts learning French. Although he knows very few words, he regards himself as a hotshot with pronunciation. He tries to teach his landlady how to pronounce 'bon'. 'It's bon, bon, as in Bondi,' he insists, but she can't get it 'right'. Tony daydreams he's a Frenchman, complete with a beret and striped matelot shirt, sitting at a white wrought iron table, Gitane cigarette dangling from his lips. A hand enters shot and pours him a glass of wine.

A suave Tony performs an elaborate tasting ritual then looks up at the pourer and says 'Bon'. The camera pulls back to reveal his landlady, dressed as a French waitress. She replies 'bon' in her 'bad' accent. The scene ends on a close-up of one of Tony's 'innit marvellous, you can't get the staff these days' looks before he snaps back to reality.

To avoid problems with rubberneckers, we shot well before the Sydney morning rush hour. Filming went smoothly and we finished quite quickly. Tony ambled off to his makeshift dressing room inside the King's Cross Waxworks. After he'd changed the manageress offered him a personal guided tour.

One exhibit featured an aborigine known as One Pound Jimmy, so named because every time he was asked to do even the simplest task, he'd always say: 'One pound, boss.' Tony turned his eyes heavenwards. Cleopatra, Marie Antoinette, Jezebel, and five other femmes fatale left Tony cold. His interest was aroused by the Jolly Swagman, where Tony discovered that 'humping a bluey' meant carrying one's Waltzing Matilda, a type of kit bag, and that a jumbuck was a baby lamb. He moved away rolling his tongue round those words, digesting them for future use.

The appalling conditions aboard a convict ship which had once transported petty criminals to the Antipodes was depicted in a gruesome tableau, in which a sadistic ship's master, one Captain Trail, is discussing the condition of the latest immigrants with Governor Philip. There are dead or dying men, women and starving children everywhere. In the foreground lay a filthy, unkempt convict dressed in rags, his face covered in grotesque pustules. A giant rat is eyeballing him, with a view to a snack. The manageress had earlier told me that this figure was a recycled likeness of Kenneth More. I asked Tony if he recognised the face. He stared at it for a few moments and said, 'Stone me, it's Kenny More... Wait 'til I get back,' he chortled, 'and tell him where he's wound up.' Then he stopped laughing, nodded thoughtfully and said quietly, almost to himself, 'It's tough really, to think what can happen when you fall from grace.'

Our location sequences were quickly processed and edited into a rough cut – the first trial joining together of the film to see how it shapes up. When the men in suits viewed it, they loved it and cheerfully increased the first batch of programmes from six to 13 episodes, with the possibility of another 13 after that.

It wasn't until 1997 that I discovered just how cock-a-hoop they were. Hugh Stuckey had been invited to a private board room party attended by Jim Oswin, the Chairman and others after a screening. 'They were very pleased with it, they were thrilled with it and they commissioned me – Oswin did this in front in front of other executives,' Hugh assured me, 'they commissioned me to write the second thirteen episodes alone. They cracked a bottle of champagne, and I was the hero.'

Good ideas began bouncing around. The scripts were moving along nicely, thank you. Hancock was working and working well. It looks like Hancock Rides Again. We were back in business.

16

The twentieth century was too much for him

Dry rehearsals for studio filming began on 3 June.

As Tony was tiring quickly I didn't rehearse him all day. He was probably working ten times harder than ever before, but his new-found determination to actually memorise his scripts came to naught.

The Hancock method of learning lines was to audio tape-record the entire script, except his own bits, for which he'd leave blanks on the track by silently mouthing his lines. He'd then play it all back and try to speak his words over the spaces. It seemed a good idea, except that he always had problems with machinery of every kind, and despite his protestations that he was good with them – 'Of course, I can work a tape recorder,' he alleged, 'I've had two of my own' – his method didn't work. The missing brain cells were wreaking their vengeance.

Tony was the exact opposite of a technocrat. He had a phobia about everything technical. It wasn't just gadgets and machinery he couldn't come to terms with, his sense of direction was uncannily poor. When he got out of a lift, for example, he'd inevitably go the wrong way, even if he'd been in the lift umpteen times before. An almost infallible method of finding one's way in an unfamiliar place was to take the opposite direction chosen by Tony.

The twentieth century was too much for him.

He seldom managed to open car doors on his own and when he did, it would invariably be the one on the wrong side of the road. He'd simply get out and wander into the traffic, and in this respect he had led a charmed life. I came to think of him as a Victorian who'd been transposed from that era to the 1960s. In that incarnation he'd have been the guy who carried the red flag in front of the diabolical horseless carriages.

Occasionally, on the way home, when time permitted, we'd visit the 729 Club, named for two commercial television channels, Seven and Nine, and the Australian Broadcasting Corporation, Channel Two. Here Tony could be relatively sure that the professional TV folk who frequented the place would pay him far less attention than he'd get most anywhere else, so he became very fond of the 729. The one-arm bandits fascinated him. They're called poker machines in Australia, and we both enjoyed gambling on them. When I ran out of change, I'd watch him taking a fiendish delight in feeding them handfuls of coins. Once, when he ran out of change and we had to go, he told me: 'I beat it this time, I only lost a quid.'

I had serious doubts about Tony having enough stamina – which was directly proportional to the quality of his performance – to carry him through the exceptionally busy schedule, particularly since he was on newly prescribed sedatives.

To lessen his learning difficulties we prepared three sets of cue cards, so that no matter which camera angle we used (he could not be certain to remember which camera we planned he should play to) the cards would be there for him.

This procedure further complicated matters because extra scene hands were needed to hold them. Mechanical prompters were out of the question, and not only on a cost basis. They simply could not be attached to the huge film cameras.

The pilot programme had taught me many lessons and because of the continuity problems encountered with it, I looked into the possibility of obtaining a feed from the E-CAM's electronic pictures to a video recorder. This would enable us to immediately judge whether or not the scene was acceptable artistically and technically, without waiting 24 hours to check the processed film. Most importantly, it would allow Tony himself to see what he was doing wrong and to correct and improve his performance as and when necessary.

125

Today, many motion pictures are shot with the aid of 'video assist' – an electronic camera attached to the film camera to allow the production team to see exactly what they are shooting *during* shooting and indeed, to review what has been shot at any time. The E-CAM system was devised for this purpose, but the electronics were quite primitive.

In 1968 the microchip was still science fiction and the tiny viewfinders built into our Arriflex cameras were barely adequate on close ups and medium shots. On wide angles, the poor-quality monochrome picture did not allow cameramen to precisely judge whether or not they were shooting off the set. The pictures on the control-room monitors were larger than those on the viewfinders, but even less distinct. Unlike electronic television cameras, the E-CAM viewfinders could not be accurately adjusted to allow operators to carry out the director's precise framing requirements. Nor was it possible to distinguish microphone shadows, lighting flare, make-up subtleties and other important details.

These were the days when two-inch-wide video tape was standard on all professional video recorders. They were considered far too expensive for ATN-7 to tie up a VTR machine – and its operator – for our two full days a week usage. VHS and Betacam were years away from general use. The only low-cost recording machine available was the Philips VCR, a relatively cheap trailblazing home video recorder.

This device would, I argued, also save money because the flawed takes on film would not need to be processed, and, planning for the unexpected, the video recorder would eliminate having to re-shoot anything for any reason at a later date, when sets would have to be re-erected and performers recalled. No, said ATN-7. What, I asked, if the artists were no longer available? The question was dismissed with a shrug.

Although one engineer insisted that the Philips recorder wasn't compatible with E-CAM's electronics, the fact was that by the time shooting restarted on *The Hancock Show*, so much money had been spent that every expense incurred was being subjected to microscopic scrutiny. Another engineer felt confident that, given a few days, he could modify the equipment. This request was turned down flat all along the chain of command right up to Managing Director level. It was hinted that the requirement was frivolous and a luxury.

Result – no video. A decision which was to cost them dear in the end.

17

'There's been an accident'

When we all moved into the house at Birriga Road improvements to Tony's sparsely furnished flat began immediately, and we quickly made him comfortable. Necessities were provided by the landlord as well as the ATN-7 props department. The seasons are reversed down there, and June was midwinter in Oz. It was very chilly at night and in the early morning. Tony complained about this, and the studio promptly installed a couple of large industrial electric heaters which were normally used to warm up the studios on cold mornings.

The telephone company promised VIP service. The usual wait, they claimed, was several months, but as it was for Mr Hancock, they'd hurry it along despite the backlog, and we wouldn't have to wait more than 'a few weeks'.

This obviated the possibility of alarm calls for Tony, and my wife devised a method of ensuring that he woke up in the mornings without anyone having to brave the weather by going downstairs to his flat. It was a solid house and shouting would have been a waste of time, so on days when Tony wasn't needed at the studios, we'd leave him to waken in his own time, but if he had to be up for work, we'd bang with a shoe on the floor of our bedroom which was directly above his. Tony'd bang back on his ceiling with a broomstick to signal that he was awake. Simple. Cheap. Effective.

On Monday night, 24 June, my wife and I had a dinner date with friends. Tony was invariably included in the many invitations

128

we received, but he politely declined this time because, he said, he wanted to study his script.

That day's rehearsals finished at about four in the afternoon. Tony looked exhausted. I wanted to discuss future casting with him, but he asked if we could do this another time as he wanted to go home. Normally I would have driven him home with me, but there were still matters which needed my attention at the studio, so a cab was ordered for him. I accompanied him to the foyer where we said goodbye. It was the last time I saw him alive.

When Tony reached Birriga Road he dropped in to see my wife. They had coffee and a chat. He made a few phone calls and left when the babysitter Mary Flod and her friend Suellyn Price reported for duty.

My wife takes up the narrative: 'We got home after midnight and Mary told us that Mr Hancock had come knocking at the door at about 8.30 p.m., asking if we were home. She had informed him that we'd gone out to a party. He'd said, "Oh yes, now I remember." And left.

'The following morning I woke up early as I had to get our eldest daughter, Lynn, ready for a school trip up the Paramatta River, a name indelibly inscribed in my brain.

'It was a pretty day. Cold with a pretty sky, a typical winter's day in Sydney.

'I banged on the floor as usual but didn't get any response. A few minutes later I banged again and still had no response. I was now getting three children ready for school and had to wake Eddie up as well as Tony.'

That morning, 25 June 1968, I had a minor hangover and my wife's admonitions – 'Get up you lazy so-and-so' – were largely ignored while I tried to sneak a few extra minutes' sleep.

My wife was in more of a hurry than usual and she was understandably crotchety. 'You'd better go and wake Tony, he's not up yet,' she said.

I suggested she send Lynn, our eldest, downstairs to do just that and my wife said, 'She's not ready, she's still having her breakfast.'

129

I fell asleep.

My daughter Lynn takes up the story: 'I remember the events leading up to our going to Australia. The most significant thing was the day Tony Hancock died. My ninth birthday was just a few days away. We were living in a house built on two levels, with a long stairway going down the side of the house down into the garden. I'm told we called him Mr Helicopter, but I don't know why. I do remember being slightly intimidated by him but not scared of him.

'He was distant, he was unfriendly from a little child's point of view. He was very unresponsive to us kids as I recall. The thought that he was a comedian always confused me because he was such an unhappy-looking man. I knew he was famous but I didn't know to what extent. I knew my dad was making a television pro-gramme with him, but that's all.

'Of course we knew Tony Hancock was staying with us, and we always had to be quiet. It was "Shhh, don't disturb Mr Hancock." He was an intruder in our house in a way.

'He didn't play with us. He didn't speak to us. I actually don't even remember much about Tony Hancock except as a presence, a shadow. I wouldn't have remembered him and, had he not died, he would never have made a lasting impression on me.

'I sometimes went down to that flat in the morning to give him a wake-up call. This particular morning I was sent to wake him up. I knocked but there was no reply. That door was slightly ajar but not enough to see into the room – it was open just a crack.

'I remember knocking and knocking and knocking. My curi-osity as a kid would have been to go in. I wasn't scared of him, I was scared of going in.

'That memory probably wouldn't have stayed with me if I hadn't been at my friend Ruth's that afternoon. There was a news item on television, and there was Tony Hancock's face. I said to my friend: "That's the man who lives with us." She said, "Oh rubbish." I said: "It is, it is, it is him!" The newsreader said this man was dead. I kept telling my friend that he was the man who lived with us, but she didn't believe me.'

Lynn had a tough time in Sydney: 'I remember sort of growing into Australia. I remembered it not being cosy in the beginning. I was bullied because I had a strange accent. Kids are horrible at eight ... I had cat's-eye glasses ... it wasn't a great time for my self esteem.'

Not all Lynn's memories were quite so traumatic, and she can recall many of the good things: 'I remember the thrill of living in the same suite as the Beatles. Mummy took us to all the Sydney sights. Once she almost dragged us up Rose Bay hill to look at the sunset. She said, "Look at the sunset," and we said, "Yes Ma, yes Ma." She said, "No, you must look at this, you'll remember this." And I do.

'When as an adult, I saw the video of the special Dad made in Sydney, I thought – hmmm, he must have been better in his heyday, because to me, and I love British comedy, it wasn't a consummate performance.'

As her father, I am, and always will be, thankful that Lynn didn't go into that room on that fatal day.

Myrtle said: 'When Lynn came back a few minutes later she informed me that Tony wasn't answering her knock. At this point I absolutely had a convincing vision of something untoward downstairs. I told her to watch the other two while I went down myself.'

My wife had twice broken her leg the previous year, and it took her a while to negotiate the unevenly paved steps down to Tony's flat.

'I knocked on the side door. There was no response. I hobbled to the front door. As I came round the corner I was aware of an aura of death.

'I didn't go into the room and I scrambled back up the stairs. I told the kids to get into the car and woke Eddie.'

My wife rushed into the bedroom. She looked terrible and was very distraught. 'Something's wrong,' she gasped. 'You had better get downstairs. Quickly!'

I knew Tony was dead before she finished her sentence. It must have been the combination of the look of horror on her face, her pallor, the urgency in her voice, whatever. I pulled on a pair of trousers, grabbed a shirt and rushed barefoot downstairs and into Tony's room. The first thing that struck me was the intense heat from the industrial heaters, which had been left on all night. Tony lay on his back across the bed. He wore only a pair of underpants. His right leg was bent upwards, his left leg dangled over the edge of the bed. In his left hand was the stub of a filter cigarette burnt down to his fingers, the ash all over his hand. In his other hand was a ball pen. His eyes were open. Vivid blue. Staring. At his side lay an empty half-jack bottle of vodka. Pill bottles, full and empty, were everywhere.

I touched him, intending to shake him, hoping, I suppose, against hope, that he was simply resting before getting up. His body was ice-cold despite the industrial heaters still on full blast. Next to him on the bed was a copy of the script we were due to shoot in three days' time. The back of the last two pages had been used to write two notes, both addressed to me. I tried to read them but couldn't focus on the content. I went to pieces and remember weeping and asking, 'Why Tony, why?' out loud, a number of times. I don't know how long I sat on the bed with Tony. I was truly traumatised, but I knew I had to do something positive and I forced myself to try to think straight. I took the notes, turned off the heaters and went back to my flat.

The first and last times I saw Hancock were in amazingly similar surroundings. Spartan accommodation, no pictures, few books. Only this time Tony didn't even have that giant teddy bear for company.

My wife had left of course, and taken the children to school.

The first thing I did was telephone the police: 'There's been a death here, a suicide.' They asked who it was, and I said: 'You'll know when you get here.'

I was certain Tony's death would make headlines and my thoughts turned to his mother. I didn't want Lil Sennett to hear the news from the media, so I immediately telephoned her in England.

Mrs Sennett and I had often spoken to each other on the phone, and we'd become quite friendly. I'd kept her up to date on Tony's progress before, during and after his spell in the hospital. It was

132

early morning in Sydney, so UK time was about 6 p.m. Mrs Sennett answered the telephone.

'Hello Mrs Sennett,' I said, 'it's Eddie in Sydney.' I wanted to break the tragic news to her gently, but I was unable to come up with anything better than: 'There's been an accident.'

Tony's mum made it easy for me when she said, 'Tony's dead, isn't he?' It wasn't really a question, more a statement of what she must have gleaned from my tone of voice.

I told her I hadn't wanted her to hear the news on radio, TV or from the newspapers. I related, as best and as calmly as I could, a brief outline of the events leading up Tony's death. She listened silently, asking only a few questions. I read her both Tony's suicide notes.

The first one said:

> *Dear Eddie*
> *This is quite rational please give my love to my mother, but there was nothing left to do. Things seemed to go too wrong too many times*
> *Tony*

The other:

> *Ed –*
> *Please send my mother this, I am so sorry to cause her any more grief as she has already had enough – but please pass on this message to her – that the soul is indestructible & therefore Bill, who means nothing to you will understand.*
> *Please send her my love as deeply as possible...*

The writing now becomes indecipherable.

Bill was a medium in whom Lil had great faith. It looks as if some of her deep interest in spiritualism must have had a profound effect on Tony to move him to write in these terms as he lay dying.

Lil Sennett thanked me for looking after him and for caring for him. Although she was deeply upset, she didn't sound very

Dear Eddie
This is quite rational
please give my love to
my mother, but there
was nothing left to do.
Things seemed to go too wrong
too many times .

Tony

Ed —

Please send my mother this, I
am so sorry to cause her any
more grief as she has already
had enough — but please pass on
this message to her — that the
soul is indestructable and ∴
therefore Bill who means nothing to
you will understand.

Please send her my love as
deeply as possible

Boeast, mother body
my — he will send to you
g on single elf
this to her code

surprised and, judging by the way she spoke, it was as if she had expected something like this sooner or later.

Our house was rapidly besieged by hordes of people. Until that day I didn't know that the Sydney media monitored police calls, and it seemed like minutes after my emergency call that the media descended in droves. Fortunately, the ambulance and the police beat them to it by a short head and kept most of them at bay, except for one photographer who sneaked through the cordon into the flat to grab a shot of Tony's bedroom.

My wife broke the Sydney speed limit all the way to drop the children, and she returned home in record time: 'I raced to the school hoping that some traffic cop would follow me, but boy, they're never there when you want 'em. By the time I got back to the house, the ambulance, police, reporters and TV film crews had arrived.'

Nearly 30 years later my wife reminded me that I had told her I thought Tony may have left a message on his tape recorder. She said that after identifying the body for the police, I'd wanted to listen to Tony's recorder but found the tape had spooled off the reel and lay scrunched up on the floor. I had no recollection whatever of this, but it seemed logical that a simple matter like that may possibly have triggered Tony's final curtain call, and my wife's guess is that when the machine played up, Tony had come upstairs to seek my assistance in fixing it.

She put it this way: 'When we weren't there for him and he got back downstairs, he realised that he was not going to know his lines the next day and everybody would have thought that he was drunk again. Who knows what happened from then on?'

She might have been right. It might have been something as spontaneous as that. Tony was like that – he loved spontaneity.

Joan Le Mesurier takes a different view: 'He hadn't heard from me, you see. He hadn't got my letters, so he really thought we were finished as well,' she told me. 'He was completely on the skids and there was nowhere else to go. And he was just depressed. I mean, he suffered from depression when he was sober. He used to sit and look out of the window for hours. You couldn't speak to him. You couldn't go near him.'

136

These moods overwhelmed him during his dry-outs.

Joan's opinion is that: 'He bought the vodka not to get drunk, but to wash down the pills with the thought "If I'm going to go, I might as well do it with vodka rather than water."'

When I asked her if Tony had ever discussed suicide, Joan told me it was only ever in the context of Freddie's various attempts. Tony put it this way to her: 'If anybody wanted to die, it's very easy. You don't try to kill yourself – you make sure no one's there to interrupt you and you do a good job. If I ever do, I shall only do it once, I'll get it right the first time ...'

I was very surprised that Tony hadn't left any messages for Joan in the notes he wrote to me when he was dying. Nor did he address anything to her on his deathbed, but, it seems, he had already written his farewell to her. In her book Joan quotes one of Tony's last two letters to her received shortly before he died: 'I loved you more than I thought possible, but now I realise that you never shared this feeling. I now relinquish you to your own life and will forget you in time. You admonished me many times about wasting my life. Now I say the same to you. I shall not brood over you. In a few weeks our relationship will be dead, cold and unremembered.'

In the other letter she received on the same day, he wrote: 'My love, my love, what else is there to say but this, just hold on to the fact that we will be together in time.'

'There was nothing for me,' Joan said in her book, 'I had already received mine.'

18

'It just seemed to be a case of when'

Although Tony commanded fabulous fees at his peak during the glory days at the BBC, no one, apart from him, his agents, the taxman and the Beeb knew quite how much he earned. He was very evasive about his income. On the *Face to Face* interview eight years before his last stand in Australia, Tony had coyly denied earning over £30,000 a year – a breathtaking fortune in those days. Even today, in the late nineties, my bank manager's estimate puts the figure at nearly £400,000. Nevertheless, in 1968 Tony considered he was on his uppers. During his torrid first year with Joan, he'd endured no less than 16 detoxification attempts so that a hefty percentage of his capital had been poured into those 'cures' and down his throat. Add the cost of his incessant international phone calls, his seemingly boundless generosity to his mother, and the escalating legal fees from a top law firm in relation to his divorce, and it's easy to understand his deep concern about money.

Tony brooded about Lil Sennett's financial welfare, which was no doubt magnified in his mind since his 74-year-old mother had recently sustained a fall, hurting both legs and bruising a rib. Tony was worldly wise enough to know that, as a woman scorned, Freddie would take him for every penny she could, and the divorce was juggernauting towards the courtroom.

Tony's mum was also broke at the time. She wrote to him, saying she'd withdrawn her last £300 from her building society to book a Mediterranean cruise. Mrs Sennett was 'Mad on cruises,'

Joan told me, 'she was always going on cruises and she used to flirt with the pursers.'

Mum knew Tony would foot the bill for her cruise. She was most concerned about him, and in the same letter advising him of her finances she referred to his mental state: 'Please do not get too depressed...' she wrote, 'The anxiety is enough to make one ill and your living is so important.'

On 9 July, from the *Chusan*, a cruise ship 'nearing Naples', Lil Sennett wrote me a pensive letter in reply to my letter of sympathy to her. 'I only wish I could talk to you personally when perhaps you could enlighten me on the cause of his tragic end. I just cannot realize he is not still with us and what we meant to each other. He phoned me in the morning telling me of his new address and that he would be having a phone installed and could phone me more often. What could have happened to him?'

This seemed a strange question considering she knew of Tony's ill-considered letter to Joan, telling her it was all over. He'd asked Mum to contact Joan for him, and when she was unsuccessful in reaching Joan, Mrs Sennett spoke to Joan's mother who took it upon herself to tell Mrs Sennett that Joan was abroad with John, that she was finished with Tony and that she didn't want to talk to him. Mrs Sennett passed all that on to Tony.

When I replied to her letter, I told Mrs Sennett that I preferred not to speculate in writing to avoid anything being misconstrued and unintentionally causing her any further grief.

In mid August, I received another letter, this time from 'SS *Andes* at Sea'. It was almost identical to her July letter which suggested to me that she had forgotten what she had written previously. This letter, in a far steadier hand, said: 'I am sure I will never get over my loss. When he phoned me in the morning (our time) he seemed so happy.' She went on to say, 'His doctor says he was never suicidal otherwise he would not have trusted him with so many sleeping tablets.'

Tony's mother was his sole beneficiary. There was £22,467 in his estate. Freddie was awarded £11,500 which was £5,000 less than her counsel had suggested to the court. In his judgment, Mr Justice Buckley said Mr Hancock owed his wife 'a moral

139

obligation of a very high order' because of the disruption the marriage had caused to her business, social and domestic life.

The last months of Tony's life held a series of contradictions. On the plus side, he appeared to be on the mend. At the very least he seemed to be winning his fight against alcohol. He had an apartment he liked and his umbilical cord – a telephone – was on its way. His life, which centred around his work in Australia, was looking promising.

In the studio the time came for Tony to be let loose in the kitchen ('kitsch-en' would be more apposite), which, in the words of his landlady, was 'a push-button paradise'.

Tony relished his exploration of that push-button paradise in which nothing quite worked the way it should, the landlady's late husband having been mad about do-it-yourself.

Sod's law and an art director with a mild case of amnesia dictated that Percy's Push Buttons were knobs instead of buttons, but it was too late for any set modification so we pressed on regardless. Without dialogue, Tony could again concentrate on his business.

Each time he twiddled a knob something unexpected happened. The first switch on a large control panel caused the telephone to move away, then back again. Tony watches, fascinated. The next knob opens a broom cupboard. Tony moves to another panel above the cooker. His twist produces music. Puzzled, he tries to fathom out the source and finds it originates from a cooker. A cooker knob tunes in a radio station playing a classic harpsichord harp piece which is not to Tony's taste. The next knob provides muted beat music, which he prefers. He lifts a kettle on a hob and the volume increases. Tony reacts to the rhythm.

Another control releases an ironing board from a cupboard. Tony replaces it and closes the cupboard door, but the board falls out once more. He returns the board, closes the door and waits expectantly, hands ready to catch it when it falls again. It doesn't. Pots cascade from a high cupboard with the next knob. Tony plays Nureyev-esque football with them until he trips. Yet another twist of the wrist operates the toaster, which immediately coughs out slices of burnt toast. Tony gingerly removes one hot slice and

140

juggles it towards the flip-lid, foot-operated, pedal bin, into which he drops the toast. This sparks an idea. He experiments with the lid a few times before tapping a cup on the worktop to ensure it's plastic. He drops the cup on to the bin lid in an attempt to hit the cup back up into his hands, but this doesn't work and the cup falls harmlessly to the floor. He has another go, and this time the cup bounces back up and he catches it. Magic. Smug satisfaction. Delighted with his skill, he tries it again – with an untested china cup – which of course smashes on the floor.

This flip-bin catching scene might have taken a thousand attempts if we'd had to do it for real, but I had to be sure it worked first time, which it did, because we simply ran the film backwards in post-production creating the illusion that Tony had, at long last, learnt to co-ordinate his limbs.

Glimpses of Tony's old comedic excellence shone through this short sequence which ran under two-and-a-half minutes. The confidence, the timing, the facial expressions, the mugging to camera – here was the genuine Hancock at his best. Well, almost.

'On Saturday,' Clare wrote, 'we were in the studio from eight in the morning till eight in the evening, but it was quite a successful day.'

The first three programmes were indeed quite successful, again with the caveat of comparison with the pilot – and despite Tony's reliance on the idiot boards, his performance kept improving – ever so slightly – as we went along.

On 18 June 1968, one week before Tony's suicide, I approved payment for 13 scripts, subject only to minor rewrites. The next day I issued the production schedule taking us to 21 September 1968.

There seemed to be no apparent reason for him to doubt he could make a comeback. Booze permitting. But another 23 shows loomed ahead. Did that frighten him? He knew what a responsibility he was shouldering. He knew that a large number of people depended on the series, on *him*, for their living. Did that depress him? Did he know he was finished professionally? Was he aware that he couldn't begin to retrieve the dizzying success of his Hancockian heyday, when his television audience reached a

141

fantastic thirteen-and-a-half million people. Had he really passed his professional sell-by date? If the series was successful, would it be acceptable in the USA? Were the ghosts of his father and his brother and his dead brain cells haunting his skull?

Did he think of the enchanting, flaxen-haired child at the Sydney Show Ground? Did he consider the effect his overdose would have on his loved ones, particularly his mother and Joan?

Did he decide on suicide before he went to the off licence to buy that half-jack of vodka? Or did he take the final decision when he returned to the flat, bottle in hand, his entire being crying out for a slug and, having done that hearing the echo of the chairman's warning to shove him on 'the first bloody plane back to Blighty'?

So many questions. So few answers.

I still have the receipt from the Bottle Department at Hotel Bondi for $1.67 worth of vodka... Whether the purchase was premeditated or spur of the moment, it made no difference, that sales slip was the signature on his death warrant.

After calling the police on that grim morning, I rang Clare Richardson. This is what she wrote to her parents on the following day, 26 June 1968: 'What a tide of woes I have to relate! No doubt the news reached you almost as quickly as it hit Sydney, I was perhaps the 3rd or 4th person to know. I was just about to leave the house at about 8.15 on Thursday morning when the phone rang. It was Eddie, completely inarticulate and sobbing terribly. He just told me to come, so I had an anxious drive with all sorts of imaginings running through my head ... and I thought that either his wife or one of the children must be dead. For some reason I didn't even think of Tony, so it was a considerable shock to find his body being carried out in an ambulance, and to be told he had committed suicide.'

On her arrival, I asked Clare to break the news to Jim Oswin, ATN-7's MD, and to Dusty Nelson to ensure that all production activities and schedules were immediately halted.

I declined to make an official statement to the police until after I had recovered some measure of composure and had time to muster my thoughts. The house was full of rozzers, ambulance men and sundry hangers-on. My wife phoned a doctor, who came

142

round immediately to give me a jab which knocked me out for hours.

Although my wife's day had also been blurred she insists she has 'absolute recollection' of frequently going to the door to dismiss Press people asking about Hancock and/or Joffe by pretending they'd come to the wrong address.

'A lot of people from the studio came round. Although Hancock was a friend to all of them, he was also their meal ticket, and that had abruptly ended.'

Myrtle seemingly retained her cool, but as Clare Richardson wrote home: 'She was in a state of suspended shock and talked incessantly, and even sang and played on her guitar.'

'At about four o'clock,' my wife remembered, 'when we'd all cried ourselves out for the day, we went to a restaurant to eat, as we'd had nothing all day. I remember the incongruity of sitting there and seeing a tabloid newspaper which someone had left behind. The whole page had two huge words and a picture on it. HANCOCK DEAD. In a way it did not surprise me, his death. I think perhaps I had always felt that this man was on a road to self-destruction.'

Tony's leading lady, Gloria Dawn, was driving to rehearsals when she heard the news on her car radio. She narrowly missed a serious crash as she swerved off the road in shock.

Eleven thousand miles away, Beryl Vertue also heard the news on her car radio: 'I remember thinking of him over there away from any of us, and it sounded so pathetic and lonely. I fidgeted a bit, wishing he hadn't been so lonely. Maybe we should all have stayed with him. I wasn't surprised, but I'd always felt, I don't know why, but I felt that his life would have a very unhappy end. It just seemed to be a case of when, really.'

There had been nothing about Tony's behaviour at any time to suggest to me or anyone else working with him in Australia that it was remotely possible that he might attempt to take his own life. He enjoyed discussing life and death, but the word suicide never entered the conversations except in those passing references to Freddie's attempts, yet few people who knew him were surprised when it happened. Shocked, yes. Surprised, no.

A typical reaction came from Catherine Freeman, who said she and John Freeman were: 'Disturbed at his suicide, but not terribly surprised.'

Alan Simpson: 'I mean it was very sad, but I can't say I was surprised. No, saddened. Saddened because it was such a terrible waste.'

Hugh Stuckey, Mike Wale and I had once speculated on what might eventually kill Tony. We discussed liver failure, alcohol poisoning, accidental OD. Neither old age nor suicide entered the equation.

Hugh Stuckey: 'I was sure he'd set fire to himself or the bed. When we were at the Travelodge (in Sydney) I had the room next to him, and that's what made me his keeper, and I used to sit with him until last thing at night – I was there Monday to Friday.

'I had a key to his room,' Hugh recalls, 'and I'd always check that he was still alive in the morning, and I used to go around last thing at night and try and find the bottles. I thought I knew all his hiding places, but there was one that fooled me and it turned out that it was in the cistern, so he'd always wake up every morning with a bottle.

'I thought he'd burn himself – he always had burn marks on his chest where the cigarette had fallen out of his mouth. Quite often his singlet would be smouldered. Oh yeah, I saw him every morning, so I can assure you that's true. And the other thing of course, he had the famous old Qantas airline bag and that had all the pills in it. At about four in the morning he'd say, "Ohhh, I think I'll have green ones tonight," and he'd grab four green pills and whack 'em down with a glass of vodka. That's how I thought he'd die.'

I wish I could remember who wrote a wise summing-up of the reason Tony had killed himself. It went, if I remember correctly, 'He couldn't stand the thought of trying to stay sober to endure the burden of everyone's expectations.'

I asked one of Tony's closest friends, Philip Oakes, why he thought Tony had done it: 'Despair. Despair. Absolute despair. I think he knew he'd never, never get back there. That's booze. It was the booze that did it. It was the booze that did everything. That was the root cause of every one of Tony's ailments.'

The police were still there, I'm told, when we returned home after that meal. They had left all Tony's drugs behind. When I later telephoned them to ask what to do with the pills, they advised me to flush them down the toilet, but something made me photograph the contents of Tony's airline bag before pulling the chain on them. Tony would doubtless have sported an extra large grin at the thought of what might happen to any passing sharks wherever the sewers discharged into the ocean.

Shortly after Tony left hospital, I'd asked the ATN-7 Press Office to subscribe to a press cuttings service which charged per cutting delivered. Tony's death triggered a deluge of cuttings from almost every English-language newspaper outside the USA. Most papers carried the news in banner headlines. In the UK Tony's death wiped out other front-page news. Cuttings poured in from the UK, Canada, New Zealand, South Africa and the Australian papers.

Magazines and newspapers printed stories claiming that Tony had been well on the way to renewed stardom. The tributes were unstinting. The *Sydney Daily Mirror*'s editorial was probably the most succinct. 'We can be deeply sorry for his unhappiness,' it said, 'but not sorry that the same stresses which finally overwhelmed him were the inspiration for the exquisite comedy of *Hancock's Half-Hour*.' Exquisite comedy. Tony would have relished that.

19

'One can only admire his fortitude'

ATN-7 whinged at the unexpected expense generated by the quantity of articles from all over the world.

Everyone under the sun, it seemed, had been a fan of Tony's, and dozens of people who'd only met him fleetingly or simply glimpsed him in the street suddenly claimed intimate friendship or became tribute-makers to a talented star. They were almost all interviewed by the media, who doubtless hoped that one of them might provide another Hancock headline.

On 29 June, the day on which we had been scheduled to complete Episode Four, about 150 people gathered in St Martin's Church in the posh Sydney suburb of Killara to pay tribute to Anthony John Hancock, Comedian.

'It was a cold, bleak day, and a very very sad affair,' Clare recorded, 'all the people who had worked with him here attended, but it was a poor offering to a man who had made millions laugh. The service was low-key and not very inspired, except for the reading of Corinthians 13. I hadn't heard or read it for far too long, and I found it very moving. I think it would be hard to rival it with anything else ever written.'

Martin Collins of *The Australian* wrote: 'It was, in a way, a final glorious joke; solemnly sending off a rare common man amid such elderly gentility – mansions, wood smoke, dreams of retirement...' And this was merely the cold confirmation of a death we had felt so deeply. So we weren't too emotional – we just wanted to pay tribute by attending.'

From the aborted pilot 'Sleepless Night'

An exhausted Tony arrives at his Australian hotel (© Seven Network – Australia)

The house at Birriga Road, Bellevue Hill, Sydney. Bottom left is the bedroom in which Tony died.

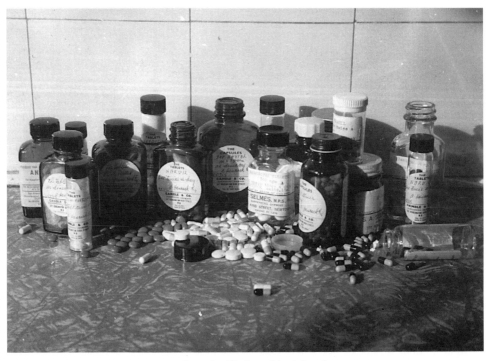

Most of Tony's pills from his airline bag.

Possibly the most poignant message was attached to some beautiful flowers: 'To a sad clown,' it read, 'whose sadness is now contentment.' It was unsigned.

After all the hymns had been sung, prayers recited and eulogies completed, some of us adjourned to a nearby hotel to drink a final toast to The Lad Himself.

I don't remember seeing John Collins there.

Willy Rushton, the well-known English comedian, was in Australia at the time, and we gave him Tony's watch to return to Tony's mother together with Tony's ashes. When he boarded the aircraft clutching the container, he told the crew Tony Hancock was in it. With due deference, the crew insisted that the ashes should travel first-class. As all cricketers know, after every Test Match series between Australia and England, the victors are deemed to have won the Ashes. How proud and delighted Tony would have been at the glorious thought of the Ashes returning to England. Even if they were his.

A post-mortem was compulsory and my wife and I had to make statements, as did the babysitters. I took a lot of time preparing mine to ensure that I only provided essential details. My statement went:

'On April 9th, 1968, I arrived in Sydney to work with Tony Hancock on a new television series. He was drinking very heavily at the time and his work was suffering. As a result he volunteered to go into Cavell House Private Hospital at Rose Bay for a rest. He stayed there from April 20th until about May 10th. When he left Cavell House he went to stay with friends at Killara. After my family and I moved into the house at 98 Birriga Road, he came and took up residence in the garden flat. Whilst he was living at the flat he was in close contact with us and was regarded as a member of the family. He would come and go as he pleased and would retire to his flat for privacy.

'On Monday June 24th we finished rehearsals at about 4 p.m. Afterwards there were details of production to be discussed but Tony was tired and wanted to go home to learn

his script. I still had work to do and ordered a cab for him. The last time I saw him alive was when he entered the taxi.

'It was our practice to bang on the floor in the mornings to waken him. He would generally respond so we would know that he was awake. If there was no response someone would go down to ensure that he was up. On the morning of Tuesday 25th June, we banged at 7.30 a.m. and again at 7.45 am. At about 8.15 a.m., before leaving to take my daughter to school, my wife went downstairs to make sure that Tony was awake.

'I was dressing at the time and my wife dashed in and said, "Something's wrong, you had better get downstairs quickly." I hurried down, found the main door locked and went around to the garden door which was open. I found Tony lying on the bed. I tried to wake him but he was dead. Then I went upstairs and telephoned the emergency service for the ambulance and police.

'From the time he left hospital he remained teetotal. To my knowledge he did not touch any alcohol until the night he died. During this period he had a lot of problems in his personal life and although he was working well, he was tiring easily.

'Later I went back to the flat with Sergeant Soane and identified the body of the deceased as being that of Anthony John Hancock.'

The inquest itself was held at 10 a.m. on 4 September. I don't remember much about it either, except that the coroner asked me to speak up so everyone could hear. I didn't do that. I didn't want to parade my sense of grief or provide intimate details for the benefit of the sensationalist Press.

The coroner summed up sympathetically: 'Looking at the background,' he said, 'and the worries that beset him, one can only admire his fortitude in carrying on his work and giving pleasure and enjoyment to others when he himself was beset with problems in his own private life. It is true these problems finally overcame him. Suicide is not a disease, a crime, or a sin, but a symptom of many different problems, ranging from chronic mental illness to an impulsive solution, or occasionally a more planned solution to a crisis in an individual's life.'

The official finding declared: 'Anthony John Hancock died from the effects of an overdose of amylo-barbitone, self-administered while affected by alcohol while he was in a state of severe mental depression.'

As Tony said himself '... there was nothing left to do. Things seemed to go too wrong too many times.'

LATE FINAL EXTRA

No. 19,194   TUESDAY, JUNE 25, 1968   Five cents

THE SUN

Telephone 2-0944. Jones Street, Broadway. Letters to Box 506, G.P.O., Sydney, 2001.

HOW TO MAKE AN EXTRA DOLLAR
TURN TO PAGE 12

● City forecast: Dry. Moderating wind ● Lotteries: Special 1626; Ordinary 6042, P. 34 ● Finance, P. 48 ● TV, P. 47

TONY HANCOCK DEAD IN FLAT

TONY HANCOCK

BRILLIANT English comedian Tony Hancock was found dead in a flat in Birriga Road, Bellevue Hill, today.

Hancock, 43, is believed to have taken an overdose of sleeping tablets. He left two notes, one of which said, in part, "Give my love to my mother."

His body, clad only in underwear, was found on top of a single bed by a TV producer who lives in the same building.

Hancock is believed to have been depressed since the weekend when he received news from London that a divorce decree against him had been made absolute.

CONTINUED ON PAGE 2.

SEX IN SCHOOLS, Page 32

THE AFTERMATH

The ATN-7 executives were once again caught on the horns of a dilemma. What the hell do we do now? they asked themselves. The decision to end the series had been taken from them by Tony's final act. We can no longer pretend it'll be all right on the night and fob off the world's Press with stories that Tony is unwell, suffering from exhaustion or whatever... Ask Ed, they said. Ed didn't know either. He was reeling from what happened. OK, OK, let's call in some wise men and we'll all look at it they say.

Although I knew they wanted to salvage something, anything, from what we had, I was too close to it and wanted, indeed needed, feedback from fresh minds.

So a rough cut was assembled and a screening of the three episodes was organised, to which executives from ATN-7's film arm, Artransa Park Film Studios, were invited. The idea was for them to view it 'cold' without any explanations of what I thought could or should be done with it. The only preamble came from my film editor, John McPhail, who wanted to make a few technical points.

The lights dimmed. The first screening of *The Tony Hancock Show* began. About 90 minutes later when the lights went up, there was nothing but silence in that small preview theatre. No one spoke a word. They were all stunned into this eerie quiet, the sort of tangible silence that prevails when one swims underwater wearing ear plugs.

151

I hadn't wanted to turn the screening into a talking shop and had requested written critiques, preferably constructive, about the material they viewed, and whether or not they felt it might be aimed at the big screen as well as TV.

These are some of the comments:

> *'I enjoyed it very much and I can't see that it would help greatly to add anything or to take much away. Perhaps it's just the pathos of Hancock but it did leave me feeling very sad. I don't think there's much that can be done about this.'*

'This production might be saved by the use of a commentator – perhaps Chips Rafferty or Bob Monkhouse. The few flashes of genuine Hancock that come through could then be properly cut without padding except for the integration of some Australian scenes.'

> *'Briefly, I cannot see how they could make anything of feature use out of the segments shown unless it is in the form of an autobiography with a story written around this type of production.'*

'I found this film entertaining because to me personally Hancock was a very entertaining man, and I felt emotionally involved probably because I had worked with him. This may or may not cloud my thoughts. In general I feel this film would be better for television release rather than cinema as it is an obvious close-up television technique. There are obvious cuts which undoubtedly would be filled with other shooting. Parts of the dialogue and action are definitely Hancock humour but this is not everyone's cup of tea. At the moment the film does not come to any logical conclusion – I feel there is a beginning, a middle and no end. The majority of the cast do not quite match Hancock's ability in acting. Mrs Gilroy was very overplayed as was the housemaid, although the housemaid had more personality impact.'

'I think the Tony Hancock Shows *must be converted to a TV special rather than a film for cinema for the following reasons:*

'1. There are too many really slow sequences that would have to come out of it anyway to make it anywhere like feature-length unless it was padded with material that did not contain Hancock.

'2. It is completely TV in its make-up. Short sequences such as the wrong girl being invited to his cabin, the drinking session at the Leagues Club etc. are OK for a half-hour TV show but there is no story line running through throughout to maintain your interest as a good film must have.

'3. It seems an impossible task to write an ending without the star. As it is it has a start, a middle of some sort and no end.

'4. If it were made a TV Special, the very fact that the man is dead and that this was an effort at comedy by a man who was mentally spent must double its interest.'

'Overall I see it as a mixture of the old Hancock who of course was masterful, some sequences where he looked, and no doubt felt terrible, some where the gag lines were so spaced it seemed they would never arrive. I liked specially the football and racing sequence and the performance of Gloria Dawn (the amorous land-lady). The drinking session at the Leagues Club was a beaut [*sic*] idea which fell away to nothing. The cooking sequence was quite the worst and was typical of how he fell away when he was on his own. When the gags were good, he was good, when they weren't he couldn't help them. Provided it was really well written I think it would make an excellent TV oncer. I can't see it as a film at all.'

'I enjoyed the film, being a fan of Hancock's for many years and am sure the public would appreciate it despite the continuity bridges which, of necessity, are at present rough. The addition of ripple dream dissolves and the forward and reverse printing of several shots which were represented by opaque spacing (as explained by the film editor) should smooth out the continuity somewhat ... I thought the amorous

153

landlady sequence very funny.... The addition of music and sound effects will do much to build up the film and an opening or closing memorium [sic] to Tony Hancock would seem in order. Could this be delivered by say, Sid James or some well-known artist who Hancock has worked with? Could this sequence be shot in England? The film would make a good TV special, after all the public know the tragic passing of Tony Hancock and would look forward to seeing his "final curtain call". As to theatre release I would hesitate to give an opinion. I think it possible with a lot of additional shooting and dressing up. Hancock's technique of delivering lines to the camera may seem a little strange to theatre audiences but who knows, it could start a new trend.'

'My approach to this screening was one of considerable anticipation because I have always enjoyed Hancock both on radio and television. However, I would say I was disappointed in the overall picture although I enjoyed quite a number of sequences. My opinion is that Hancock was always funnier when he played to another character, he seemed to have lost his touch of being at his best during his "monologue" sketches...

'The most appealing things were the flashbacks to leading the players on to the field and the racing interlude. Do I think the material could be made into a feature film? Not without a lot of rewriting and shooting to provide better links between sequences.'

'I feel that the pace is too regular and episodic to sustain interest as a 1½ hour feature as it stands. Although most sequences are very funny indeed, I felt the kitchen sequence was a little contrived and overlong. However, no doubt sound effects will help this a great deal.'

In other words, the wise men felt, this was for the box and not the cinema. I was too disorientated to make value judgments at that time. But the wise men had made valid comments which helped me get my mind back into gear.

154

I worked on a feasibility study, and felt that *if* we could find a suitable double, and *if* we filmed linking shots, and *if* we reshot certain key scenes possibly using a voice-over narration, it *might* somehow work as a television 'special'.

The decision to try a salvage operation was taken and planning began on ways and means of turning the two and a half episodes into a 'special'.

The first three programmes were more or less continuous. Episode One, 'The Journey', was about Tony's voyage across the oceans. The second programme, 'Home', began with Tony's first conflict with Australian bureaucracy in the form of an awkward customs officer. He then encounters the staff of a sleazy hotel and is referred to the widow's apartment. The title for Episode Three, 'In Search of Friends', gave him the opportunity to cross swords with a bunch of sports-mad Aussies.

I was fully aware of serious continuity errors in these episodes. In the normal course of events, they would have been rectified by reshooting the relevant sequences as soon as the schedule permitted.

For example, a key shipboard scene in Tony's cabin in Episode One is preserved, as it were, on celluloid amber, on the dreadfully emasculated copy of the *Special* released on video. In this scene, Tony sends a note to a glamorous young woman, inviting her to his cabin for dinner. He has Mervyn act as his valet-cum-waiter to impress her. To Tony's chagrin, Mervyn delivered the letter to an elderly spinster with the same surname as the dolly bird . . .

Nevertheless Tony isn't one to waste the dinner. When the meal ends, Tony pours the coffee while chatting away. So intently was he concentrating on reading his cue cards that he accidentally poured the coffee into the cream jug instead of a cup.

When he failed to get the action right after three or four stabs at it, I decided not to risk a repetition of the pilot fiasco, so I moved on to a different scene with the intention of reshooting the cabin scene at a later date.

Altogether about 15 per cent of the content of the new shows needed 'pick-ups' to remedy Tony's mistakes.

In the case of one vital scene which was essential to the story, we would be forced to enlarge the entire sequence because the wide-angle camera was positioned too far away from the set, revealing the edges, thus destroying the illusion of being in a customs shed. We knew the quality would be ghastly because enlarging motion picture film stock produces a grainy, out-of-focus amateurish 'look', but there would be no alternative because Tony featured in each and every angle shot in that shed.

After weighing up these and other problems, I told the management that they were again facing grave risks trying to make a special, but they said go for it regardless. So we did.

To try to iron out other major continuity problems and to have a 'Hancockian presence' in the exterior establishing shots, we had first to find a double. Eventually we settled for an actor called Roy Waterson, who vaguely resembled Tony. From behind, that is. His hair and build were roughly similar to Tony's and, most importantly, Roy almost got the Hancock walk right. Wearing the Homburg and astrakhan, there was a passing resemblance, but only in extreme wide-angle long shots.

There was never any intention to ever see the double's face, but we did not anticipate a problem with the back of his head – the ears, to be more precise. Tony had odd ears. They were quite large with a rubbery look to them, so a pair of prosthetic false ears were made for use in those scenes which required the 'presence'. Roy was filmed from behind, pointing the camera at the person talking to him.

The film editor with his editing machine was on the studio floor throughout the filming sessions to allow us to double-check continuity and to aid actors and cameramen to more easily replicate what they had done during the original filming.

Months of dedicated, painstaking labour went into getting that *Special* right. Or as 'right' as we could. I knew we were on a hiding to nothing in terms of turning it into a tearaway success, but I was determined to make it as polished as humanly possible to hopefully ensure that Tony's final effort did not sully his professional reputation.

It was therefore essential to examine every foot of film we'd shot, including unprocessed takes previously regarded as NG (no good) to see if even tiny sections could be utilised to improve the *Special*.

We also played back the audio track of lines Tony had delivered. Roy mouthed these silently to give the slight head movement people make when talking. This also gave the other actor something to react to while listening.

Another example of the care lavished on our thankless task was in a kitchen scene where Tony is trying some gourmet cookery. He reads the recipe out loud. The lines were, 'Bring to the boil on a low oven ... A low oven? No, I think I'll cheat, I'll use the top.' In the best take Tony had said low in the first sentence and 'slow' instead of 'low' in the second sentence, thus killing any possibility of a laugh. We substituted the word 'low' from another take but that didn't work, so the 's' from the good take was painstakingly removed by the editor. And it worked. Little else went so well.

The filming sessions, with the double dressed in Tony's clothes while hearing Tony's voice, were downright macabre and everyone in the studio became very depressed. It seemed that there was a presence of some sort around when we were shooting. Malignant may be too strong a word, but things never seemed quite 'right' for any of us. In the end none of the double's dialogue sequences were usable, and the only scene in which he appears as Tony in the final product is in a montage of him wandering through Sydney lugging some heavy suitcases.

Much as I dislike manufactured laugh tracks, there were some awful silences on the sound track which had to be filled. I had considered screening the fine cut for an audience to gauge where best to fit the laughs and what sort of laughs to use. When you think about it, there are inordinate types of laughter, ranging from titters (assorted), belly laughs, whoofers, guffaws, giggles (small, medium and large), chortles, chuckles, sniggers, to half-started laughs, convulsive laughs, hysterical laughs, irritating laughs, derisive laughs, screaming laughs, jeering laughs, nervous laughs, musical laughs, laughs of relief, delayed laughs which come seconds after the personal penny has dropped. The list goes on and on. An audience also coughs, clears its throat, fidgets, sniffs, sneezes, wheezes. Try listening carefully to the next situation comedy audience show on TV, and judge for yourself. During the Artransa screening we'd recorded a guide laugh track, which proved useless because the audience had been too numb to react. I feared this might happen again, even with a hand-picked audience of Tony's greatest fans. We'd run out of time so we had to press on and trust our instincts.

For me one of the most satisfying stages in the production process is when the music is added to the sound track. Good music, carefully chosen or composed, is very important, and our music director Tommy Tycho, did a splendid job. Being present at the sound recordings with a large professional orchestra was a joy. The Hancock theme and incidental music were top class and added a new, fresh dimension to the production.

But even this could not rescue our *Special*.

No one engaged on the *Special* expected it to work. And we were right. When it eventually reached London, a preview was arranged for various senior television executives, including Jeremy Isaacs, then Director of Production at Thames Television. Everyone present agreed that it was light years away from the high standards Tony set at the BBC. It was almost as if the man on the screen was a lookalike trying to imitate Hancock. It was only ever transmitted in Oz, and nowhere else.

The Tony Hancock Special
The Complete Post Production Script

<u>T O N Y   H A N C O C K</u>

by

HUGH STUCKEY

With additiohal material by
MICHAEL WALE

PRODUCED & DIRECTED
by
EDWARD JOFFE

AN ATN - 7 COLOUR PRODUCTION, FILMED IN SYDNEY, AUSTRALIA.

161

CAST

Mervyn .... DON CROSBY
Miss Bancroft .... GEORGIE STERLING
Mrs. Gilroy ...... GLORIA DAWN
Milkman .... LEX MITCHELL

ON BOARD SHIP

Captain .... KENNETH LAIRD
Ent. Officer .... DON PHILPS
Bandsman .... BRIAN BARRIE
Bikini Bancroft.. MIMI DIXON
Boy .... MARSHALL CROSBY
Colonel .... EDWARD HOWELL

ON ARRIVAL

Customs Officer . DON REID
Hotel Clerk ..... MAX PHIPPS
Landlord .... NAT LEVISON
Man in Pub....... JAMES ELLIOTT
Maid .... DOREEN WARBURTON

LEAGUES CLUB

Herbie .... KEVIN LESLIE
Ken .... GRAHAM ROUSE
Pete .... ROGER WARD
Chips .... BRIAN NYLAND
Barmaid .... MAXINE WYATT

With

Bettie Crosby
Christina Daniel
Patsy Flanagan
Ron Golding
John Hilton
John Hopkins
Maudie Jacques
Bob Karl
Joanne Neville
Stan Nicholls
John Quinlan
Roy Waterson

CREDITS

Director's Assistant ....CLARE RICHARDSON
Assistant to the Producer ......DUSTY NELSON
Floor Manager ....PETER MACDONNELL

Art Director ....WILLIAM WELLS
Designer ....WALLACE LOGUE
Properties ....LAWRIE LYNAGH
Construction ....HAROLD TAYLOR
Set Dressing ....NOEL BECKETT
Graphics ....RON JUBB

Casting ....FRANZ CONDE
Editor ....JOHN MCPHAIL

Wardrobe ....RAY WILSON/WYNNE NEBAUER
Make-up ....VAL SMITH

Location Cameramen ....GORDON GRIFFIN/DON CLAY
Unit Manager ....ALLAN MEWTON
Continuity ....PAM PUNCH

Audio ....WESTON BAKER
Lighting ....BOB FLETCHER
Camera Operators ....DOUG HAMPSON/MURRAY POLLARD
                               PETER MOSS/JOHN PARTRIDGE
Technical Director ....RAY HANCOCK

Music ....TOMMY TYCHO

162

SCENE 1

Shot

1.."Seven" Ident	Fanfare
Ident zooms back to compass of old map	Music
Truck in towards England	Voice over mu: ic
2..MS COOK	Two hundred years ago
Sailing ship	James Cook set forth from England to seek and enticing new land called
Ship bobs up and down waves	'TERRA AUSTRALIS'
Cook looks thru' telescope	upon which to plant ....
Truck into Union Jack behind Cook.	'THE FLAG'

3..Dissolve to LS British Isles.
Modern cartoon ship tugs to
release itself from bollard,   To emulate the traditions set by
eventually pulling England
away from Scotland, sails round the EARLY EMPIRE BUILDERS,
globe, England in tow, flag
prominent.

4..Cartoon Hancock looking thru' INTREPID ENGLISHMEN, FOLLOW TO THE
binoculars   ANTIPODEAN COLONY TO THIS VERY DAY.
Superimpore "TONY HANCOCK"
                                  MUSIC UP

5..Ship continues to sail round
globe. It is now upside down.

6..Sails into Great Australian Bight
which becomes shark-like mouth.
This closes, chews boat and
England, hiccups out Union Jack,
Hancock Homburg Hat.

Truck into flag.

Superimpose "Written by Hugh Stuckey"

Flat flicks lettering off·
Superimpose "Additional material
by Michael Wale"

Lettering flicks off.

Superimpose "Produced & Directed
by Edward Joffe"

                                         FADE OUT   1.04"

COMMERCIAL BREAK   - OPTIONAL

SCENE 2

<u>Shot</u>

1... Bow Waves   MUSIC

2... Seagulls

3... L.S. SHIP AT SEA

SCENE 3 DECK OF LINER.   DAY

1... LS. DECK. STEWARD ENTERS   MUSIC & F/X
     WHISTLING CRAB L + HIM TO
     DECK CHAIR. HE COLLECTS GLASSES
     EMPTYING DREGS.

2... M.S. STEWARD EMPTYING DREGS.

3... LS CAPTAIN DESCENDING STAIRS.
     NOTICES HIS HAND IS DIRTY FROM
     RAIL. WIPES RAIL AGAIN. EXAMINES
     IT. WALKS IMPERIOUSLY IN
     DIRECTION OF STEWARD. STEWARD
     NEARLY BUMPS INTO HIM.

4... CU CAPTAIN REACTION

5... M2S CAPTAIN STEWARD. CAPTAIN
     REMOVES ORANGE SLICE FROM
     GLASS,DRINKS GLASS, COUGHS,
     RAISES EYEBROW, GIVES STEWARD
     DISDAINFUL LOOK.

6... CU STEWARD OBSEQUIUS REACTION.

7... MLS STEWARD CAPTAIN. CAPTAIN
     LEAVES. STEWARD HEARS APPROACHING
     MOB. WITH A DOUBLE TAKE AT DOOR,
     HE GRABS A GLASS FROM DECK CHAIR
     AND VANISHES SMARTLY.

8... LS DECK
     DOOR BURSTS OPEN AND MOB APPEARS.
     CRAB AS TONY TRIES TO GET A DECK--
     CHAIR. A YOUNG COUPLE TAKE 1ST
     CHAIR. COLONEL JUST BEATS TONY
     TO NEXT CHAIR. PAN R. AS TONY
     MOVES FOR THIRD CHAIR, BUT A
     BEAUTIFUL BIKINI GIRL IS THERE
     FIRST.

9... MCU TONY
     TONY REACTS

10.. LS TONY INCLUDING OLD LADY
     AN OLD LADY HOBBLES JUST AHEAD
     OF HIM.

11.. MLS TONY FRONTAL CLAMBERING
     TOWARDS CHAIR PAN +HIM. OLD
     LADY SEES HIS INTENTION. SHE
     JABS HIM WITH HER WALKING STICK
     AS SHE IS ABOUT TO SIT. SHE
     APPEARS TO lIFT HIM WITH STICK

12.. MCU TONY'S PAINED EXPRESSION   <u>TONY</u>   A tough old bird like that
                                     ought to be able to stand up all day.

13... MLS TONY CLAMBERS TO LAST CHAIR
      BUT EN ROUTE A FAT WOMAN GOES FOR
      CHAIR THEY STRUGGLE FOR THE CHAIR

14... MCU AS THEY STRUGGLE

WOMAN   Excuse me .... Sir ...

TONY   There you are I hope you're
satisfied now we've both missed it.

15... LS DECK TONY COMES TO RAIL

There's nothing I'd enjoy less right
now than standing up here getting
burnt to a cinder. There are times
when I really think that now every
Englishman is worthy of carrying Her
Brittanic Majesty's passport...Look
at 'em.. rolling about there. A whole
nation of sitters...that's what became
of us. It makes you wonder about
evolution...If the human body develops
those parts that get the most use,
well I'd like to be in England in a
couple of hundred years and I'd put my
money in seat covers. Yes that's all
that's left of the bulldog spirit
as far as most people are concerned.
Of course, we Hancocks always have
been a seafaring race. It if hadn't
been a question of time I'd have
sailed across single handed. But
life's too short to fit everything in.
It's all right for Sir Francis
Chichester, but I've got too much on
me plate. I've got to help build up
a new country. After all Captain Cook
didn't arrive single handed did he?..
I wonder if Matilda's still waltzing
around with that kangaroo?

16... M2S TONY, MERVYN ENTERS.

MERVYN Hallo Hancock. Thought you
might like a pint.

TONY Have you any idea what time it
is?

MERVYN (LOOKS AT WATCH) Yer, it's
about six o'clock. That'd make it
ten o'clock in London and in Hong
Kong .....

17... CU TONY

TONY It is the cocktail hour. And
you bring me a pint of crudely iced
beer wearing what I can only describe
as totally informal dress. At the
cocktail hour, be it in Bombay or

Brixton people should be properly
attired.

18... M2S FAVOURING MERVYN

MERVYN Just because you've only got
one suit.

19... M2S FAVOURING TONY

TONY As we near your former home in
the Antipones Mervyn, I deduce signs
of you getting above yourself.

20... FRONTAL 2S

Remember you have been in Britain
for the past six years and our
influence throughout the world is
built upon a tradition of observing
social rituals such as the cocktail
hour. Now kindly go and get properly
dressed.

MERVYN It's no good living in the
past, Hancock. They won't put up with
all that class bit over there.

TONY Oh won't they? Huh, we'll soon
see about that. Oh, yes. (TAKES
PASSPORT FROM POCKET, BRANDISHES IT)
see this, I'll have you know this is
a British Passport...have you ever
read what it says inside?

MERVYN Eh?

TONY Right.

21... MS TONY

EASE IN TO CU

her Brittanic Majesty's Principal
Secretary of State for Foreign requests
and requires in the name of Her
Majesty all those whom it may concern
to allow the bearer to pass freely
without let or hindrance, and to
afford the bearer such assistance
and protection as may be necessary.

MUSIC OUT.

22... MCU MERVYN

MERVYN I'd like to hear you read
that mouthful if you were in a punch-
up in Wagga.

23... M2S TONY, MERVYN

TONY You're forgetting, Mervyn, the
guards never retreat. LOOKS AT WATCH
Well, as it's nearing the end of the
cocktail hour, just a minute lets have
a go. DRINKS MOUTHFUL. Don't think
much of that.

24... MLS

Shot

24...	MLS	TONY Ugh.

OFFICER HANDING OUT INVITATIONS TO
PASSENGERS. MUMBLED THANKS.

25...   CU OFFICER OUT TO 2S
       TONY/MERVYN
     TONY WATCHES THE INVITATIONS
     BEING HANDED OUT.

TONY   Oh! Its ridiculous the way
they're handing round cards with our
position and altitude on.

MERVYN   That's only on aeroplanes

TONY: Well ...depth... position of
iceburgs and other natural hazards.

26.... 2S, INCLUDE OFFICER IN B/G

MERVYN More than likely he's handing
out invitations for the Captains
Dinner, this is the last night at sea
and they always invite anyone who
hasn't dined dined with him so far.

TONY Ah, that's a point. I'll have
to get changed. I wonder whether I
should wear the tails or the MCC
blazer.

       OFFICER JOINS TONY AND
            MERVYN
     ADMIT OFFICER PAN L. TO 2S
     TONY OFFICER LOSING MERVYN

OFFICER

Hallo there. Making the most of
your last day at sea?

TONY Oh yes. Hallo there yes.
Nothing like the old ozone.

OFFICER   Oh no.

TONY   I hear it's fried seagull
again. The Captain's favourite dish.
Ha, ha, ha...

OFFICER   Oh no. It's a bit special
tonight what with having to select
the two millionth migrant.

TONY   Ahhhhhh, yes. (THINKS IT'S
HIM).

OFFICER   It's quite a distinction.

27.. CU MERVYN

MERVYN Are we all eligible....?

28.. 3S OFFICER TONY MERVYN

OFFICER   Well originally. But there
have been elimations.

TONY (LOOKING AT MERVYN)
Some are automatic.

OFFICER   Yes, wel, um, its all going
to be settled at dinner tonight.

MERVYN   Have you got an invitation
for Mr. Hancock?

TONY   Ah, he's probably left it in
the cabin.

OFFICER   (LOOKING DOWN LIST)
Oh dear, well I'm afraid your name
isn't on the list. Yes. Well I must
be getting along you know, lots of
preparations for tonight. Ho! well
cheerio, see you later, ha ha.

TONY   (SOURLY)
Yer, I bet there are.

OFFICER LEAVES   MERVYN   Oh, you're not missing much.
Pretty stuffy these affairs. It's
probably just an oversight.

29.. MCU TONY   TONY   Oh no it's not. It's a
deliberate snub from the Captain. I
didn't like the look of him from the
moment I stepped foot on board. Looks
like a Greek to me. Probably got the
only lifebelt on the ship stowed away
under his bed. No doubt I have been
a little outspoken on his handling
of the ship. But there aren't enought
people these days who will speak their
minds - risk their future. Too many
people are content to hide behind the
organisation. It is the age of the
anonymous man and I am not annnymous.

30.. CU MERVYN   MERVYN   As far as the Captain's
concerned, you are.

31.. 2S TONY MERVYN   TONY   No matter. Be that as it may.
MISS BIKINI IN B/G   I shall have to use my initiative.
Make my own plans. A small soiree in
my cabin. Just an intimate affair.

MERVYN   Who with?

TONY   Well who better than Miss
Bancroft over there? A splendid
GIRL EXITS   example of feminine pulchritude.

32.. MCU TONY REACTION
33.. O.S. 2S FAVOURING MERVYN   MERVYN   Do you want us to dress
formally?

34.. O.S. 2S FAVOURING TONY   TONY   No just wear your white jacket..
you know. That one you bought at the

Army and Navy Surplus Stores...

MERVYN   And Miss Bancroft?

35.: FRONTAL 2S

TONY   As much as I admire her curvacious grace and slimline beauty I must insist that on this occasion she is - fully clothed.

MERVYN   I shall issue the invitation formally immediately. (MERVYN LEAVES)

IN TO MS TONY

TONY   Aye, aye, Mr. Mervyn.. I said all along the wrong man was running this ship.

24.. FADE-OUT

MUSIC PLAY OUT.

END REEL 1

6.17"
(From Bow waves)

COMMERCIAL BREAK

R E E L 2

1... BILLBOARD

MUSIC

SCENE 4   TONY'S CABIN   NIGHT.

2... FULL SHOT PORTHOLE SLOW OUT TO
LS TONY

TONY   I bet Captain Bligh had a bigger cabin than this. That's the trouble of being a £10 migrant. They take advantage of you. I expected at least a State Room. After all they want me out there. Oh yes.. they need people like me out there. It's lucky my great grand-father Admiral Hancock isn't alive to see this. He'd have a fit. A seafaring personage like myself confined to a dog kennel like this. It's a wonder they didn't put me in chains or lash me to the mizenmast.. or funnel, or whatever they do these days. (LOOKS AT WATCH)
Hello it's coming up seven bells I'd better get changed.

TONY STEPS INTO WARDROBE
CLOSES IT.

3.. MCU WARDROBE DOOR
ONE ARM COMES OUT IN BLUE
BLAZER. DISAPPEARS. OTHER ARM
COMES OUT.

MUSIC

4... MLS CABIN. CABIN DOOR OPENS MERVYN ENTERS.	MERVYN Hancock, Hancock.
TONY COMES OUT WITH TWO BLAZERS ON	Oh I delivered the invitation, slipped it under Miss Bancroft's door.
	TONY Good, good.
	MERVYN Oh hold on, I'll give you
MERVYN HELPS TONY INTO MCC BLAZER	a hand.
	TONY Be careful, careful. It's a very choice piece of clobber. Ha, Ha, that's more like it.
	MERVYN (TOUCHES MCC BADGE) MCC?
5... CU BADGE OUT TO 2S TONY MERVYN FAVOURING TONY	When did you work for the Manchester City Corporation?
	TONY The Manchester Ci.... This is the Marylebone Cricket Club. You've heard of Typhoon Tyson, you're looking at hurricane Hancock.
6... M2S TONY MERVYN	TONY They're very proud of this badge in my family. I'm sure it will impress Miss B.
MERVYN SETS UP TABLE	MERVYN Yes very impressive.
	TONY That's better.
	MERVYN Oh, we'll need another chair.
	TONYNo you won't have time to sit down, just ah, get the table lad. (CROSSES TO GRAMOPHONE) Right now, what shall we have.
7... MS TONY SORTS RECORDS	TONY Shall we have Noel Coward, or Land of Hope and Glory? MERVYN I prefer Rolf Harris. TONY Yes you would.
8... MLS TONY, MERVYN	MERVYN Where would you like Miss Bancroft to sit?
TIGHTEN TO MS AS TONY CROSSES TO MERVYN	TONY Over there beneath the porthole. Lit from behind she would look a rare beauty. I shall also be able to view her more easily. Mervyn, I needn't stress too strongly that I'm relying on your discretion this evening. I'm sure you'll know when the moment has come in which to make a discreet exit.

And if you don't sense it you'll get
a good three inches of pointed patent
leather in your posterior.
TIMID KNOCK

MERVYN GOES TO OPEN DOOR
TONY STOPS HIM.

TONY   Hold, listen to that gentle
knock.
MERVYN   Oh Hancock you're that
romantic. (ANOTHER FIRMER KNOCK)
TONY   There's only Keats and Shelley
and me left.
Open the door, Mervyn.

MERVYN GOES TO DOOR
9...MS DOOR
DOOR OPENS TO A DIFFERENT
MISS BANCROFT.
ZOOM IN TO CU MISS BANCROFT

BANCROFT   Mr. Hancock?

10..O.S. MS TONY

TONY   I think you've got the wrong
cabin.

11.. MLS CABIN

BANCROFT   (SWEEPS INTO CABIN)
Oh, how sweet. I got your invitation.
Nearly missed it though. It got
jammed under the door.
TONY   It is MISS Bancroft?

BANCROFT   That's right, but my
friends call me Bunny, actually.

12..MCU MERVYN
13..MCU MISS BANCROFT

MERVYN   Is it your daughter
the one in the bikini on the sundeck?
BANCROFT   Oh no. I gather we've got
the same name, but that's all we share
in common.

14..MCU TONY

TONY   You do not exaggerate.

15..MLS

BANCROFT   Um do we sit or stand for
aperitifs?
TONY   Mervyn, Mervyn!

16...MS TONY, MERVYN

MERVYN   Is this the moment when you
want me to leave you?
TONY   No, you foo. We want the
aperitifs.
MERVYN   Aperitifs? What's that?
TONY   Sherry Sherry, that's all we've
got, the Sherry.

17...LS CABIN

Do sit down Miss Bancroft.
BANCROFT   Oh thank you Mr. Hancock,
TONY   You must, you must, excuse my..
man. SERVES MISS B. A SHERRY AND NOT
TONY.

TONY   I will take a little sherry
tonight too, please Mervyn.

MERVYN   But there's only two glasses.

TONY   There are only two of us dining.
STEWARD KNOCKS AT DOOR AND BRINGS
MEAL ON TRAY
BANCROFT   Only the other night.

TONY   Yes

18... MCU MISS BANCROFT

BANCROFT   I was dining with the Captain.
TONY   How very nice for you.
BANCROFT   Such a charming man.

19... 2S

TONY   Yes, I wish he'd spend less
time eating and more time directing the
boat.

20... MS MISS BANCROFT

BANCROFT   Oh he's got such an appetite
brilliant man. Leads such an exciting
life.

21... CU TONY OUT TO 3S

TONY   You call that exciting. They're
nothing more or less than glorified
bus drivers. (MERVYN SERVES SOUP)
They should be on ferries if you ask
me.. All this business about dining
with them.

22... CU MISS BANCROFT

BANCROFT   Oh you haven't dined with
him Mr. Hancock?

out to 2S TONY MISS B.

TONY   No itis a mere oversight. A
A slip of the Pursers' pen.
BANCROFT   It must be very exciting
up there tonight.

23... MS MERVYN

MERVYN   Yes, I wonder who'll win the
two millionth migrant award.

24... W3S

TONY   You make it sound like a cattle
show.

25... MS MISS BANCROFT

BANCROFT   Yi know when you think about
it it's really a very great honour to
be the two millionth migrant into this
country.

26... MS TONY

TONY   Imagine letting a man like that
pick the two millionth migrant. Ha,
I, we all know about the Captain's
cabin don't we? I mean we're adults.
That's where the final decision will
be made.

27... M2S MISS BANCROFT TONY

BANCROFT   I gather he has a rather
nice cabin.
TONY   Yes, all chintz and wallpaper
I suppose. Not like Nelson.

11.

They don't make Captains like Nelson
any more.
BANCROFT   Poor man.
TONY   That's the last thing he is.
BANCROFT   No I mean Nelson. Such a
frail, sensitive person.

28... MCU MERVYN

MERVYN   My mother always thought I
looked like him.

29... MS TONY

TONY   It's the column you look like
mate, not the man. The Captain's a
fool. He hasn't got enough experience.
MERVYN WHIPS SOUP AWAY.

30... LS CABIN

TONY   Steady on Mervyn, you sure
Miss Bancroft's had enough. You're
not serving at the Captain's table
now you know.
BANCROFT   Oh, that's quite all right
Mr. Hancock.
TONY   I'm so sorry. They have to be
trained from birth otherwise they're
useless.

31... MCU MERVYN

MERVYN   If you don't eat your duck
now it will return to its original
frozen condition.

32... MCU TONY

TONY   Duck? Duck? Who wanted duck?
Perhaps Miss Bancroft would have
fancied a fillet mignon or fillet
de boeuf en croute.

33... MCU MISS BANCROFT

What say you to the Miss Bancroft?
BANCROFT   Oh no, no, no, no Duck will
do me fine.

34... 3S

MERVYN   That's good because it's duck
or nothing. MERVYN OUT.

35... MS MISS BANCROFT

BANCROFT   Mmm it's very nice.

36... 2S TONY MISS BANCROFT

TONY   No bad. Not bad. The tin foil
gets on your fillings a bit doesn't it.

37... MS MERVYN

MERVYN   Good job you had them all
done before you left.

38... 2S TONY/MERVYN

TONY   That's a point. Do you think
that the two millionth migrant gets
free medical treatment.

39... MS MISS BANCROFT

BANCROFT   Why. Do you think he'd need
it.

END REEL 2   6.33"

REEL   3

40.. MS TONY   TONY   Well, I don't mind a check
                                up from now 'til - now and then you
                                know Cholera, typhoid. Things like
                                that sort of disease is as common as
                                a cold where we're going.

41.. 2S MISS BANCROFT TONY   BANCROFT   Oh I always understood
                                it to be a very healthy country.

                                TONY   Yes possibly it is. But it's
                                the places you pass through on the
                                way, that weaken you.
                                BANCROFT   Well, I do think that good
                                health would be a pre-requisite for the
                                winner of the competition. Along
                                with all the other attributes of a
                                typical British man or woman.

42.. MS TONY   Dignity, Humility, Helpfulness..
        TO CU   the cultured sophisticated sort.
                                No doubt they've been keeping their
    RIPPLE DISSOLVE TO   eye on all of us during this voyage.

                                SCENE 5   FLASHBACK   DECK DAY

1... CU COLONEL SNORING IN CHAIR
     BESIDE TONY
     OUT TO INCL. TONY WHO IS SOUND
     ASLEEP.

2... MCU DOOR SMALL BOY ENTERS

3... LS DECK BOY ROUNDS CORNER

4... M2S BOY COLONEL.
     BOY SNEAKS FOAM AEROSOL ONTO
     COLONEL'S HAND. BOY TICKLES
     COLONEL'S NOSE. COL. BRUSHES NOSE
     IN HIS SLEEP, SMEARING CREAM ON
     HIS FACE.

5... 3S BOY, COLONEL TONY
     TONY CHASES BOY   TONY   Get out of it.
     TONY TAKES HANKY AND WIPES COLONEL'S
     FACE. THE COLONEL WAKES.   COLONEL   What the devil are you up to
                                  sir?
                                  TONY   I...I...

6... L.S.   ZOOM IN TO CU
     UNIFORMED OFFICE PASSES IN WHAT
     APPEARS TO BE CAPTAIN'S UNIFORM.
     (HE IS BANDSMAN BUT THIS IS NOT
     DISCLOSED UNTIL LATER.   OFFICER   Tch, Tch, Tch,

7... CU TONY   LOOKS GUILTY

     FLIP TO NEXT SCENE..........

<u>SCENE 6   FLASH BACK   DECK   DAY</u>

1..: CU LEGS   PAN SLOWLY UP   MUSIC
     PAUSING ON SHU-DYE.
2.,. MLS   TONY

3... CU GIRL'S HAND
4... MLS TONY
5... CU DYE, TAN LOTION
6... 2S TONY APPLIES DYE
7... CU GIRL'S BACK TONY'S P.O.V.
8... 2S TONY/GIRL
9... FRONTAL 2S
10.. CU HAND ON BACK
11.. FRONTAL 2S INTO CU TONY
12.. MLS HE RISES, SNEAKS AWAY.
     OFFICER ENTERS.
13.. CU HANDSHAKE
14.. LS TONY EXITS THRU DOOR.

   FLIP TO......   <u>SCENE 7 FLASHBACK</u>

1...   TONY LEANS ON RAIL AS BANDSMAN
       PASSES.
                          <u>TONY</u>   Oh Captain. I think there's
                          been a slight misunderstanding
                          <u>OFFICER</u>   Oh.
                          <u>TONY</u> I was merely trying to help
                          my fellow passengers. Perhaps
                          there's some little thing I might do
                          to help you?
                          OFFICER LOOKS DOUBTFUL
                          <u>TONY</u> Anything y'know just a question
                          of goodwill. Friendship. Anything
                          at all. No matter how menial a task
                          as long as we make the voyage a
                          success.
                          <u>OFFICER</u>   If you really want to help
                          Follow me.
                          <u>TONY</u>   Thank you.

   CUT TO   <u>SCENE 8   DAY   FLASH BACK BALLROOM</u>

OFFICER IS NOW REVEALED TO BE A
VIOLINIST PLAYING CZARDAS. TONY
TURNS THE PAGES OF MUSIC FOR HIM,
BUT CAN'T DO THIS RIGHT AND GETS SWEPT
AWAY BY THE MUSIC.

RIPPLE DISSOLVE TO NEXT SCENE.......

SCENE 9   TONY'S CABIN   NIGHT

DINNER IS AT THE COFFEE STAGE.
TONY IS STILL DAY-DREAMING. MISS
BANCROFT IS SLIGHTLY TIPSY ON SHERRY.

1... CU MISS BANCROFT OUT TO   BANCROFT .....I believe coffee
    2S TONY MISS BANCROFT   was invented by an Italian, although
                                   credit is given to a Benedictine Monk
                                   in the Outer Hebrides...Do you know
                                   who it was?

2... CU TONY   TONY It was the Bandsman Ha Ha yes
                                   that's right.. it was the Bandsman..
                                   it wasn't the Captain at all. Ha.
                                   ha, ha...

3... 2S TONY MISS BANCROFT   BANCROFT I can't tell you how nice
                                   it is to have found someone of my
                                   own intellectual level.

4... MCU   TONY   TONY So I still stand a chance. The
                                   prize is open. The cup can still
                                   overflow with success..

5... 2S   BANCROFT Oh yes. You're by no means
                                   past your prime and you're going to
    EASE OUT TO INCLUDE MERVYN   a new country.
                                   MERVYN He still sees himself as the
                                   two millionth migrant.
                                   BANCROFT Oh dear...

6... CU TONY   TONY I'm not the first man not to
                                   be recognised in his own lifetime.
                                   Mmm Van Gogh, Robert Louis Stevenson
                                   who invented the Rocket... Look
                                   what we did to the Germans and look
                                   where they are today.

7... W 3S   BANCROFT I I agree. It's scandalous.
                                   MERVYN (TO MISS BANCROFT)
                                   He's just jealous.

8... 2S TONY MISS BANCROFT   TONY It's all right for you but you
                                   didn't suffer. You didn't put a
                                   lifetime's work into a bed of prize
                                   marrows only to have them bombed
                                   to bits by the Hun.

9... MCU MISS BANCROFT   BANCROFT Oh, I love marrows..
                                     especially in cheese sauce. (LEANS BACK)

10.. 3S   TONY You just get used to these set
                                   backs when you're ahead of your time.
                                   MERVYN It's all this crossing the
                                   international date line. It upsets
                                   us all.

BANCROFT   Is it Mondayor Tuesday?

11.. MS TONY

TONY   No matter. Tomorrow is another day.. a new land. A man is never recognised in his own country. Even this ship is registered in London.. thus the prejudice. All this fuss over the two millionths migrant. I find it all rather plebeian really. Rather in for a dig. Who wants their picture in the papers anyway? There you are smiling away one minute and the next you're being used a a wrapper for fish and chips. Enough of my worries. The ramblings of a genius aren't to everybody's tast.

OUT TO 2S TONY MISS BANCROFT

Miss Bancroft, I apologise Madam, I'm neglecting you dear lady. Mervyn more coffee. Let's splice the mainbrace.. and have four lumps of sugar.

BANCROFT   Ooooh. That's rather fattening.

TONY   No matter. Let's lash it out. It's the last night at sea. Ah Ha sorry, there we are - it's the last at sea. The journey of a lifetime.

KNOCK AT DOOR.

12..   WS CABIN
MERVYN OPEN DOOR TO SMARTLY
UNIFORMED OFFICER.

OFFICER   (TO MERVYN)
Mr. Hancock?

TONY   Speak to him without. Miss Bancroft is in a draught.. Take a message, I'll deal with it tomorrow morning.

MERVYN GOES OUT SHUTS DOOR
TIGHTEN TO 2S MISS BANCROFT TONY

BANCROFT   I did enjoy your sherry

TONY   Yes you had a go at that didn't you

BANCROFT   Yes, I'm afraid...

13.. MS MERVYN
OUT TO INCL. TONY

MERVYN RETURNS

MERVYN   The Captain requests the pleasure of your compnay in his cabin. He wants you to join him and the other Miss Bancroft there.

TONY   Was that the Captain without?

MERVYN   No It's his right hand man.

TONY   I only speak to commanding officers, you should know that by now.

MERVYN   But Hancock this might be about the you know...

TONY   If the Captain wishes to call on me I shall be in my quarters...That is if Miss Bancroft here gives me permission to digress from out social pleasure for a moment. (MISS BANCROFT GIGGLES)

PAN L TO MISS BANCROFT LOSE MERV.
MERVYN GOES OUT OF DOOR. TONY POURS COFFEE.

BANCROFT   Lovely coffee

TONY   Yes.

MERVYN RETURNS

14... W.A. CABIN

TONY   Well?

MERVYN   He just said if you're not interested he can't wait around all night.

TONY   (STANDS)
Yes I'd better get up above... if the mountain won't come to Mohammet...

15... CU MISS BANCROFT

BANCROFT   I refuse permission. I insist you stay you darling man...

16... MLS   TONY BUNDLES HER TO DOOR

TONY   Yes Miss Bancroft thank you very much It's been a most delightful evening I've enjoyed every moment of it.

BANCROFT   Thank you. most enjoyable.

SLAMS DOOR

TONY   Yes.

17... MCU TONY

It's the best night you've ever had at sea.

18... MISS BANCROFT OVER TONY'S
       SHOULDER

BANCROFT   (POKES HEAD BACK)
I thought there might be some little way I might show my appreciation.

IN TO MCU

TONY   Heaven forbid

19...   BILLBOARD

END REEL 3

_____

COMMERCIAL BREAK

_____

REEL   4

SCENE 10

1...   BILLBOARD   -   LOCATION DAY EST. SHOTS HARBOUR.
2...   SHIP AT HEADS
3...   SMALL BOAT IN HARBOUR
4...   2nd SMALL BOAT IN HARBOUR
5...   OVER BOW TOWARDS HARBOUR BRIDGE
6...   FORT DENISON FROM SHIP

Tony applying sun cream to 'Bikini' Bancroft (Mimi Dixon). He has mistakenly picked up shoe polish instead

On location. L to R – Hugh Stuckey (writer), Eddie Joffe, Tony

A scene from the pilot episode. Tony creates a stir in the cinema when ordering a 'violet crumble'. (Beatrice Aston and Dmitri Makaroff)

On board ship, wearing 'MCC' blazer, Tony entertains the 'wrong' Miss Bancroft (Georgie Sterling and Don Crosby)

7... SIDE SHOT SHIP FROM LAND   MUSIC
8.∴ TUG
9... OPERA HOUSE FROM SHIP

    DISSOLVE TO

1... CU PRINT OF OLD SHIP OUT TO   SCENE 11 SHIP'S BALLROOM   DAY
    WS BALLROOM PASSENGERS ENTER
    CHILDREN PLAYING   HUM OF CONVERSATION

2... 2S MERVYN TONY   MERVYN How can you be sure you're
                             going to be the two millionth
                             migrant? What happened in the
                             Captain's cabin last night?
                           TONY Well we found we had a great
                           deal in common. Our interest in
                           cricket...I found him very adaptable,
                           very malleable....
                           MERVYN And corrupt
                           TONY Shhhhhhhh Here he comes.

3... MLS CAPTAIN AND ENTERTAINMENT
    OFFICER ENTER, AND WALK TO STAGE.
    INTO MS CAPTAIN. CAPTAIN CARESSES
    BLAZER BADGE SMILES KNOWINGLY
    AT TONY.

4... MS TONY   TONY ACKNOWLEDGES

5... WA BALLROOM
         (CAPTAIN'S VOICE AS OVER
           P.A. ALL THROUGH)   CAPTAIN Good morning Ladies and
                           Gentlemen.. As you are now tied to
                           the pier of what is to become your
                           new home, the moment has arrived to
                           choose the person who will represent
                           you all, and all who have come before
                           you.

6... MS CAPTAIN   Now after very careful consideration
    FAST PANL. TO MISS BANCROFT we have reduced the field to Miss
    PAN HER TO STAGE.   Felicia Bancroft (LONGUISH APPLAUSE)
                           and Mr. Anthony Hancock.

7... MS TONY HE RISES PAN HIM (SMATTERING OF APPLAUSE)
    TO STAGE

8... FULL SHOT STAGE   Now these two finalists did not
                           intrude they went about their business
                         carefully considering their fellow
                         passengers. Mr. Hancock in particular
                         was most restrained. And it was this
                         attribute I think that finally swayed
                         the judges. Ladies and Gentlemen

	your two millionth migrant (PAUSE) Mr. Anthony Hancock. CROWD APPLAUDS. Now the Press have been very very patient, they're waiting outside, would you ask them to come in Mr. Fellows.
TIGHTEN TO 3S	Congratulations
	TONY Thank you, to continue my story about Lords when I was bowling. Australia were 800 for 2 Bradman was on you know, I was bowling. My googly actually
	PRESS ENTER
	CAPTAIN
CAPTAIN GESTURES TOWARDS TONY MISS BANCROFT IS STILL BESIDE CAPTAIN AND PRESS SURROUND HER FLASH LIGHTS, INTERVIEWS.	Ladies and gentlemen, our two millionth migrant.

EASE IN TO TIGHTER SHOT GROUP

TONY   Thank you I'm very proud indeed.

(THEY IGNORE HIM, PHOTOGRAPH MISS B.)

No, no, you've got the wrong one.

10.. CU TONY

I'd just like to say how very proud I am to be the 3 millionth migrant.... It's not her, it's not her.... It's A-N-T-H-O-N-Y

11.. WIDE SHOT GROUP TONY GRABS REPORTER'S NECK.

TONY   Look mate

12... MS TONY, REPORTER PUSHES REPORTER DOWN OUT OF SHOT

TONY   It's me... it's meeee!

FADE OUT

SCENE 12   LOCATION   DAY.

1... LS SHIP OVER BAGGAGE
2... CRANE/LUGGAGE
3... PASSENGERS DISEMBARKING
4...   "   "

SCENE 13   INSIDE CUSTOMS SHED.   DAY.

1... FULL SHOT CUSTOMS SIGN. PAN
      DOWN AND LEFT,ZOOMING OUT TO
      CUSTOMS QUIUE. TONY ENTERS L.B/G

      DROPS BAGS. RUBS HANDS, LOOKS
      AT QUEUES. Q1 IS MOVING, Q2 IS
      STATIONERY. TONY JOINS Q1 WHICH
      STOPS.   Q2 MOVES. HE CROSSES
      TO Q2 WHICH STOPS AS HE JOINS IT.
      Q1 MOVES. HE NOTICES PRETTY GIRL.

LS IN MS	VOICE LOUDSPEAKER Would all migrants please have their luggage ready for inspection at the Customs counters. Thank you.
2... MS BAMBI	
3... MS TONY MERVYN JOINS HIM	MERVYN Got your luggage all ready Hancock? TONY You don't think I'm carrying this lot for nothing do you? I'm not a bedouin Arab, though under this lot I might slightly resemble a beast of burden. MERVYN They're very helpful, hardly open a case. TONY Well after all we are British. MERVYN Course they're really after the big boys. Men with a thousand watches strapped around their waist. Girls with gold tucked
4... MS BAMBI	in their bra's
5... M2S TONY MERVYN	TONY SUSPICION DISBELIEF) Can that really be all her? These Customs officers must live some very interesting lives.
6... LS MISS BANCROFT ENTERS	BANCROFT Come along my good man come along Ah hello Mr. Hancock
7... CU TRACKING SHOT	What a crowd, I had such a job to get a Porter.
8... 2S TONY MISS BANCROFT	TONY Typical never there when you do want them and always there when you don't.
9... MS GIRL & CUSTOMS OFFICER QUEUE MOVES FORWARD AS TONY GATHERS LUGGAGE. THE GIRL IS NOW AT THE COUNTER AND MISS BANCROFT EASES HER WAY INTO THE SPACE AHEAD OF TONY. CUSTOMS OFFICER OPENS GIRL'S CASE AND HOLDS UP FEMININE UNDERWEAR.	
10...2S TONY MISS BANCROFT	BANCROFT Oh really. These Customs men might have a little modesty. Is nothing sacred from the bureaucrats these days. TONY (WATCHING INTERESTEDLY) I couldn't agree more. Most embarrassing. Most embarrassing. BANCROFT I trust they won't go through our luggage like that. TONY Hmmmmm no fear of that, madam. The more mature traveller you will find

is allowed through as it states so
clearly in our British Passports;
"Without let or hindrance."

11.. L.S. GIRL IS ALLOWED THRU'

12.. CU BANCROFT

BANCROFT   (TO OFFICER)
Good morning my good man. What a
glorious day.

13.. L.S. MISS BANCROFT SIGNALS
HER PORTER THROUGH THE OFFICER
TICKS OFF HER LUGGAGE WITHOUT
A MURMUR. IT IS NOW TONY'S
TURN.

CUSTOMS MAN   Come along there. Keep
the queue moving.
TONY   (STARTING TO WALK PAST)
Good morning. Lovely day. I bet it's
still snowing in England.
CUSTOMS MAN   Just a minute.
TONY   Were you addressing your remarks
to me by any chance?
CUSTOMS MAN   What are those books?
TONY   Just a little light reading
matter. There we are a few digests,
a few condensed best sellers. I don't
have the time to read like I used to.
CUSTOMS MAN   (TAKES A BOOK)
Hummmmm. Yes, you'd be surprised what's
brought into our country under the
guise of Popular Mechanics.

14... MCU TONY

TONY   The nearest in that lot to
pornography is Little Women.

15... MLS TONY CUSTOMS OFFICER

CUSTOMS MAN   Come on. Open it all
up.
TONY   What!   All the lot?
CUSTOMS MAN   That's right. The lot.
TONY   But you let that woman through
without so much as a whisper.
CUSTOMS MAN   We become expert
character readers in our business mate..
TONY   I shall complain to the British
Ambassador about this incident.
(HOLDS OUT HIS PASSPORT)
CUSTOMS MAN   You don't need that now.
Just open the cases.

16... CU TONY

TONY   Her Brittanic Majesty will be
very angry. Very angry indeed. She's
your Queen as much as she is ours you
know. Wait till I tell her what's
going on in this colony.

17... M2S   TONY MISS BANCROFT

CUSTOMS MAN DELVES INTO ONE OF
THE SUITCASES AND TOSSES
EVERYTHIN OVER THE COUNTER. TONY Go easy. Go easy. It took
me a good hour to pack all that stuff
And my uncle had to sit on it as well.
And as I haven't brought him with me,
how we're going to get it closed up
I do not know.

18... CU TONY
   CUSTOMS MAN HOLDS UP A
   STUFFED OWL.   TONY   Family pet.

19... O.S. CUSTOMS MAN   CUSTOMS MAN It will have to stay in
              quarantine for six months.

20... CU TONY   TONY Quarantine? Six months?

21... OS CUSTOMS MAN   CUSTOMS MAN No animals or livestock
              either alive or stuffed permitted in
              without the statutory period of
              quarantine. It's not my ruling.
              It's the Government.

22... CU TONY   And I'm afraid it will cost you £5 a
              week to keep it.

              TONY £5 a week? Are you going mad
              or am I? £5 a week you propose to
              charge me for a stuffed owl that has
              been in my family for a century, in
              quarantine?

23... CU CUSTOMS MAN   CUSTOMS MAN That's the law... and a
              a matter of fact you're lucky not to
              be fined for not declaring it in the
              first place.

24... CU TONY   TONY I shall definitely petition Her
              Majesty about this one.

              CUSTOMS MAN O.K. You can go now,
              and be quick about it.

25... M2S TONY CUSTOMS MAN TONY Thank you very much indeed Sure
              you don't want the shirt off my back?
              BEGINS TO SHAMBLE OFF.
              CUSTOMS MAN Oh and by the way.....
              TONY Now what?
              CUSTOMS MAN ...... Welcome.
              TONY   (TO CAMERA)
ZOOM IN TO MCU TONY   Welcome ......

DISSOLVE TO......

           SCENE 11 LOCATION DAY

MONTAGE THRU CITY FINISHING
ON ENTERING HOTEL DUMONT.

        END REEL 4

SCENE 15   HOTEL RECEPTION   DAY   INT.

1... CU BOOK OUT TO MS CLERK
    CLERK ANSWERS.

PHONE RINGS
CLERK
Hotel Dumont. Reception. No, I'm
sorry Sir, we're full up. Migrants

    CRAB R TO SIDE SHOT FINISHING
    AS TONY ARRIVES AT COUNTER

you know. That's right, we're a kind
of a half way house for them.
CLERK   We get all types British,
Dutch, German (HE STARES AT TONY)
Cypriots.

2... CU TONY

TONY REACTS
CLERK
So sorry sir.

3... 2S TONY CLERK
    CLERK HANGS UP AND STARTS
    WRITING IN BOOK
    CLERK GIVES HIM AN INSULTING
    STARE AND GOES ON WRITING

Some other time perhaps....

TONY   Good afternoon....I was
wondering...
....I was wondering....?
CLERK   (CLOSES BOOK)
Well?
TONY   I believe there's a reservation

    CLERK STARES AT TONY, SHRUGS.

in my name. Hancock.
CLERK:
Hum.

    OPENS BOOK AND CHECKS THROUGH

Hancock....Hancock.

4... MCU TONY

TONY   Yes that's right. Straight off
the packet as you might say. Typically
British isn't it, making a voyage
like this. A seafaring race we are.
One sniff of the salt air in me lungs
and I'm all for sending a gun boat
up somebody's channel.

5... MS CLERK

REACTION

6... 2S TONY/CLERK

Yes, that's the spirit that made
Britain what it is today.
CLERK   Precisely.

CLERK TAKES KEY FROM BOARD.
THROWS IT ON DESK IN FRONT OF TONY.

TONY   Is somebody going to carry my
bags?
CLERK   Typical. Only in the country
two minutes and they expect to be
waited on hand and foot.

7... MS CLERK   RINGS BELL ON DESK.

CLERK   Boy!

8... MLS Very old man

TONY   Boy!

COMMERCIAL BREAK

1... BILLBOARD	MUSIC
2...	SCENE 16 HOTEL DUMONT SIGN CUT TO HOTEL ROOM DAY.
3... MS TONY	TONY How does one get started? Where are all those
4... MCU TONY OUT TO MS	friendly diggers who fought for us at El Alamein....? Haven't heard a person as much as whistle Waltzing Matilda yet still at least there's some Contact with the outside world.
TAKES TRANSISTOR RADIO OUT OF CASE, SITS DOWN ON BED, SWITCHES IT ON.	MUSIC.
5... MCU TONY	RADIO VOICE: (HIGH PRESSURE D.J.) Are you absolutely sure your shirt is white?
TONY CHECKS FRONT OF HIS SHIRT.	VOICE Don't be half safe. Wash your shirt in Sudso. Remember that name friends, Sudso, Sudso, Sudso! (MUSIC) TONY I'll get a packet of that. VOICE Hey, out there. It's two fif.ty three.... TONY I'll get a packet of that as well.
6... MLS TONY HE DIALS ANOTHER STATION	ABC VOICE .... were helping them in their enquiries.
7... MCU TONY	In Parliament the question of the attitude of British migrants was raised. The Minister for Immigration said that far too many people come to this country expecting everything to be done for them. Make your motto Get up and Go, the Minister said.
8... MLS TONY HE SWITCHES OFF RADIO GETS UP AND PUTS RADIO BACK INTO SUITCASE.	TONY I'll get up and go alright mate, right out of your wretched Antipodean Colony. Politicians. They're the same the world over.
9... CU TONY	They get up there and spout a whole load of codswallop.
10.. MS TONY	They've never volunteered to give up their natural born way of life. The sacrifices I've made to come here and help to put this country on its feet. Here I am all alone in this miserable

Hotel. The tropical sun beating a
tattoo on the roof. It's all
surf and seaweed here.

11... MCU THRU WINDOW
     CLOSES CURTAINS.

12... MLS   TONY

TONY (cont)
Oh, what have I done? How could
I have left all that intellectual
jousting, the verbal parry and thrust.
The comradeship

13... MCU TONY

of one's intimate friends.

14... MS TONY

Woe is me to think this time last
week I was in the ample bosom of..

15... CU TONY

(PAUSE)... the Rose and Crown.

16... MS TONY

Ahhhhh. I bet London doesn't swing any
more I've gone.

      RIPPLE TO

                    SCENE 17   BRITISH PUB INTERIOR. NIGHT

1... CU DART BOARD. OUT TO LS BAR.
    A GROUP OF MEN STAND AT THE BAR.
    THERE IS AN ATMOSPHERE OF
    CONVIVIALTITY UNTII TONY ENTERS.

TONY ENTERS SURROUNDED BY FOG.
TONY (COUGHS)
Evening all. (COUGHS) Ah,it's a bit
sharp outside tonight eh? Hello
Ena, Jim, hello Allan. Hello Geoff,
how's the missis?
MEN IGNORE HIM.
TONY   The usual please, Landlord.

2... O.S. MS FAVOURING TONY

LANDLORD   What's the usual?
TONY   Half a tomato juice in a pint
pot with a piece of lemon.

3... O.S. M.S. FAVOURING LANDLORD.

LANDLORD   Look we don't split tomato
juices. You'll have to have a couple
of them.

4... SIDE 2S TONY LANDLORD

TONY I know that. I've been coming
here for 25 years. Has Jack been in?
LANDLORD   Jack?

5... MCU TONY

TONY You know Jack. Tall feller
with the pipe, the glasses, the hat
the jacket, the trousers, the overcoat.

6... 2S LANDLORD TURNS AWAY AND
    POURS DRINK. TONY TURNS TO
    THE GROUP WHO STILL IGNORE HIM.

7... O.S. CUSTOMER FAVOURING TONY

TONY Hello lads. (UNDAUNTED, ALTHOUGH
THEY CONTINUE THEIR CONVERSATIONS
TOGETHER)
Great match at the Arsenal on Saturday
eh? See Jimmy Greaves scored another
three tries for the Spurs. That
should save them from relegation.

8... 2S TONY LANDLORD	**LANDLORD** Relegation for the Spurs? They've been in the top six for the past five years. Cor!
LANDLORD PUTS DOWN TONY'S DRINK AND TURNS AWAY IN DISGUST.	
9... MCU TONY HE TRIES HIS DRINK, SIPS AND HOLDS IT LIKE A BRANDY TURNS.	
10.. MLS TONY & GROUP	**TONY** Well this time next week I shall be in the sun leaving all you lot here shivering away in the snow and the smog. (TRYING TO ATTRACT ATTENTION) Yes Australia Here I come.
11.. O.S. CUSTOMER FAVOURING TONY	**CUSTOMER** You going to Australia? **TONY** Yes that's right. I'm getting out of all this lot. Taxed out of existence. Keeping other people in free medicine. Turning rusty in all the rain. Oh yes. I'm off. The boat leaves from Southampton tomorrow. And as far as I'm concerned it can't leave a second too soon. **CUSTOMER** (HAND ON TONY'S SHOULDER) Well in that case old man you've just got time to stand one last round of drinks before you go. I'll have a double whiskey. Nat. Come on boys free drinks all round.
12... MLS SCENE	PATRONS CROWD BAR SHOUTING FOR DOUBLE
13... MLS SCENE NEW ANGLE	SHOTS BUT THEY STILL IGNORE TONY
TONY IN CENTRE. IN TO MS.	COMPLETELY.
RIPPLE DISSOLVE TO.	

SCENE 18   HOTEL ROOM DAY

1... CU HOMBURG PAN L TO TONY ASLEEP ON BED.	
2... L.S. ROOM MAID ENTERS SINGING	**MAID** I don't want to set the world on fire. I just want to start a flame,
3... CU TONY	in your heart dee, dam,
4... LS ROOM	da, da, da, da, da, dum
5... CU TONY	da, da, da, da,
6... L.S. ROOM	**MAID** Hope I didn't disturb you sir, (PUSHES HIM OFF THE BED) Just arrived from the old country? **TONY** That's right. Just trying to settle down quietly in pastures new. **MAID** I came over in 1946, just after the War. Married myself to an Aussie soldier. It's different, of course.

7... MCU TONY	TONY Is it?
	MAID Ah but it's a beautiful country.
	Especially if you like the outdoors.
8... ML2S	We live in theoutdoors.
9... MCU TONY	TONY (APPREHENSIVELY) You do?
	MAID Well take us. We spend nearly
	all the summer on the beach. Have you
	brought your cossie?
	TONY Me.cossie!
	MAID Cossie your bathers. Your
	bathing trunks.
10.. ML 2S	OH you must do some swimming.
11.. MCU TONY	TONY I can't wait...
12.. 2S A.B.	MAID The beaches are beautifu... all
	golden rolling surf. Just like in
	the travel fims. Of course there are
	the sharks.
13.. MCU TONY	TONY. Sharks?
14...M2S A.B. MAID CROSSES TO	
DRESSER	MAID It's the Portugese Men of War
	you have to watch out for. You don't
	know they're there, see.
15...MCU TONY	TONY I won't be there either, madam.
	MAID Well perhaps you'd
16.. ML2S	enjoy pottering around the garden.
	Every home has it's little garden over
	here. We grow our own vegetables,
	at least we did.
	TONY What do you mean you did?
17.. MCU MAID	MAID Well, till the funnel webb
	spiders....
18.. 2SAB	TONY Funnel web spiders!
	MAID Yeah. They're deadly poisonous.
	They don't have an antidote yet.
	Big ugly bodies with short legs and
	they just leap out at you.
19.. MCU TONY	TONY At this rate I can't see myself
	getting out of bed.
	MAID You don't want
20.. 2S A.B.	to stay here.
	TONY (PUTS HIS FEET UP ON BED)
	Why not?
	MAID: They over charge for a start
	TONY Oh, they do do they?
	MAID Well, they don't like migrants
	yisee so the Manager says to hit them
	where it really hurts, in the pocket.

TONY   I suppose it's better than
being got by one of those what do you
call them? Funnel Web spiders Oh
what have I let myself in for? Come
back England. All is forgiven.
MAID   You want to get yourself a flat.

21.. 2S.AB.

TONY   Would they have the kind of
accommodation to which I am
accustomed.
MAID Oh better than that.
TONY   Well, actually, I was
expecting a 'phone call from my
Embassy. They're probably fixing
me up.
MAID Well, if you get stuck there's

FUMBLES IN APRON POCKET   a friend of mine. I've got a card
here somewhere - Mrs. Gilroy.
FINDS CARD GIVES IT TO TONY You never know it might come in handy.
TONY   Well thankyou that's very kind
very kind indeed. We British must
stick together.
MAID GOING TO DOOR   MAID   Ahh. We're not strictly
British any more. We're Aussies.
SHE EXITS.   TONY   Hum It's all very well for her.
22.. MS TONY   But a person with my breeding, my
heritage, my family tree. Ahhhhh.
We're British to the end. (ON BED)
So, they overcharge do they.

23.. MLS GETS UP MOVES ROUND ROOM

Well, a couple of tea towels, and an
TAKES HAND TOWELS AND ASH TRAY ANDashtray will soon settle that account.
PUTS THEM IN HIS CASE   I've got to get out of here.
24.. MCU   LOOSEN TO W/S   where did I put that card.
HE SEARCHES FOR IT IN ALL
HIS POCKETS.   Yes... Mrs. Gilroy....

END REEL 5

REEL   6

SCENE 20   THE FLAT LATE AFTERNOON

1... CU COWRIE SHELL OUT TO REVEAL
     MRS GILROY PLACING POTTERY
     HIPPO IN IT AS SHE POTTERS
     ABOUT THE DOOR CHIMES RING ..
     SHE ADJUSTS HER APPEARANCE
     OPENS DOOR TO TONY WITH
     LUGGAGE.
2... M2S   TONY   Mrs. Gilroy?
     OUT TO LS EASE IN   MRS. GILROY   URGENTLY   Oh yes,.

Come on. Come in.

TONY   The housemaid at the Hotel recommended you.

MRS. GILROY   I've been expecting you that's right put all your things down.

TONY   I've been lugging this load of rubbish half way round the world today.

3... MLS AS TONY STEPS OVER LUGGAGE.

Got blisters on me feet that raise me up so high, I'm getting nose bleeds from the altitude.

MRS. GILROY (SITTING VERY CLOSE) Oh, there, there, you poor man. Well, there's no more need for you to roam.

4... M2S

I'm sure that you'll be quite happy living here under the same roof as me.

5... CU TONY REACTION

TONY   Madam.

MRS. GILROY

6... M2S

I have the flat above.

TONY   Oh you had me worried there for a moment

MOVING EVEN CLOSER

MRS. GILROY   Oh I like to be near my tenants.

MRS. GILROY TWEAKS TONY'S NOSE PLAYFULLY.

See that they get every little thing they need.

Oh you remind me of my husband.

7... CU TONY

TONY   IS he upstairs

8... M2S   IN TO CU TONY

MRS GILROY   Way upstairs....he's dead Ho, but you're so much like him.

TONY   That's a left handed compliment if ever I hear one.

9... M2S MRS. GILROY EDGES CLOSER STILL

MRS. GILROY   Now no matter what time of the day or night if there' any little thing you need, you just call out for me. I'll be right up there listening.

10... O.S. TIGHT   - 2S FAV. TONY

TONY   Yes I can imagine, one ear up, one ear down.

11... 2S TONY MRS. GILROY

MRS. GILROY   Oh I know what loneliness can do. I'm lonely myself.

12... TIGHT O.S. 2S FAV. TONY

TONY   I'm not surprised.

13... M2S

MRS. GILROY   Every since my dear Percy passed away I've kept myself to myself.

TONY   Yes well I wouldn't want you to change your habits on my account, madam.

14... MLS TONY GETS UP

Now about this flat.

	MRS. GILROY Oh, there there, I'm rushing you, aren't I Mr. Hancock. Well never mind. I'm sure before long we'll reach a perfect understanding and I'll be able to take something off for you.
15...CU TONY	Oh, only a small
16...MLS	discount off the rent, mind you, but it all helps.
	TONY Yes, well can I just have a look at the flat?
	MRS. GILROY Certainly. This here is the lounge room and the main living area. Now through there is the bathroom hot and cold water hand basin shower recess etcetera. Oh and in here is the
GOES TOWARDS BEDROOM. STOPS. TONY DOES NOT FOLLOW	bedroom. TONY
	Yes, well, I'll have a look at that later on.
	MRS. GILROY Oh, all right. Well there is a single in there at the moment but you could change that at any time.
17... M2S PAN L + THEM AS MRS G. USHERS TONY TOWARDS KITCHEN	Don't you think it's rather neat and compact. Oh but wait until I show you the kitchen. It's got every modern built-in feature that we could think of. My Percy was a real do-it-yourself marvel ha, ha, ha.
MRS. G. UP AGAINST HIM AT BREAKFAST BAR	Spent half his life locked up in his tool shed.
	TONY I don't blame him.
	MRS. GILROY Ohh, he never had a day's tuition in his life, yet he put all the gadgets in here himself. Mad on automatic whatnots he was ha, ha, ha, This kitchen is a push button paradise, he always said.
18... TIGHT 2S FAVOURING TONY	TONY How can two human beings suddenly seem like a crowd?
19... 2S	MRS. GILROY Oh I must go and make your bed. You'll um, know where I am if you need me. EXITS.
20... CU TONY FADEOUT	
21... BILLBOARD	END REEL 5

COMMERCIAL BREAK

REEL 7

1... BILLBOARD

2...

3... CU 'CHINESE LADY' TONY REMOVES
PICTURE HANGS QUEEN VIC. IN
ITS PLACE

TIGHTEN TO CU PICTURE.

4... S 2S TONY "QUEEN VIC."

PAN WITH HIM. TONY CROSSES
TO KITCHEN TO CONTROL PANEL,
SWITCHES KNOB.

5...CU PHONE WHICH OVES. PAN UP TO
TONY STILL FIDDLING, THEN DOWN.
PHONE MOVES OPPOSITE DIRECTION.

6...CU PANEL. TONY'S HAND SWITCHES KNOB.

7...LS KITCHEN. CUPBOARD OPENS
BROOM FALLS OUT TONY STUFFS BROOM
BACK CLOSSES DOOR.

8...CU 2ND PANEL TONY SWITCHES KNOB
OUT TO MS TONY. HE CAN'T MAKE OUT
WHERE MUSIC COMES FROM, REALISES IT
IS THE COOKER, ENJOYS MUSIC, SWITCHES
KNOB. REGISTERS DISLIKE. SWITCHES
KNOB AGAIN TONY LOOKS FOR SOURCE,
PICKS UP KETTLE TONY ENJOYS MUSIC.
REPLACES KETTLE SWITCHES MUSIC OFF.

9...CU PANEL TONY'S HAND SWITCHES.
OUT TO MS TONY AS IRONING BOARD
FALLS DOWN TONY REPLACES IT
AGAIN IT FALLS TONY REPLACES IT
AGAIN AND MAKES TO CATCH IT AGAIN.
THIS TIME IT DOESN'T FALL.

10..MLS TONY HE CROSSES TO FIRST PANEL
AND SWITCHES KNOB. PANS FALL OUT
OF HIGH CUPBOARD TONY STARTS TO
KICK PANS AROUND.

11..CU TONY PAN DOWN TO FLOOR

12..MS TONY. HE ALMOST TRIPS AS HE
CROSSES TO PANEL. HE SWITCHES
ANOTHER KNOB.

13..CU TOASTER. BURNT BREAD POPS UP.
PAN UP AND OUT TO REVEAL TONY.
HE REMOVES HOT TOAST AND DROPS IT
QUICKLY INTO PEDAL BIN. PLAYS WITH
LID HE TESTS A PLASTIC CUP AND
DROPS IT INTO BIN, AIMING FOR LID
TO FLICK IT, BUT MISSES.

14..MS TONY TESTS ANOTHER CUP TO SEE
IF IT'S PLASTIC, DROPS ONTO BIN
MISSES.

15..LS TONY DROPS ANOTHER CUP ONTO LID

MUSIC

EST. FLATS

SCENE 21 TONY'S FLAT   DAY.

TONY   Oops. You looked a bit tipsy
there for a moment.

Most unseemly. God bless you Ma'am.
(SALUTES, TURNS TOWARDS KITCHEN)
I dunno the trouble with Landladies
the world over is they either want to
chuck you out, or lock you in. This
one needs a bit of watching you, Can
hardly blame her, I suppose. It's the
old charm that does it.

Now where's old Percy's push button
paradise?

F/X MUSIC

BOSSA MUSIC

DREARY HARPSICHORD MUSIC
MUFFLED BEAT MUSIC
MUSIC INCREASES
MUFFLED MUSIC

```
       IT BOUNCES UP, HE CATCHES IT AND
   .   DROPS IT ONTO LID.
16...MS. HE TAKES ANOTHER CUP DOESNT
       TEST IT.
17...LS DROPS CUP ONTO LID, LID FLICKS
       IT OFF
18...CU CHINZ CUP SMASHING
19...MS TONY   PAN HIM R. TO DOOR...   DOOR CHIMES
```

LIVING ROOM   DAY

TONY   Visitors (WALK)
I don't know anyone. Is that you
Mrs. Gilroy?
HE OPENS THE DOOR. IT'S MERVYN
TONY Oh, it's only you How did
you find me?
MERVYN   The maid at the Hotel.
TONY She's obviously got it in for me.
MERVYN   It's just that it's the first
day back...
TONY   But you used to live here.
MERVYN   All my friends have gone over
to England.
TÓNY   Got more sense than I'd have
given them credit for.
TONY PLAYS WITH CRICKET BAT.
MERVYN   I should never have gone away.

20... MS TONY O. M'S. S.   It's all different I'm a stranger in
my own land.
TONY   You're the sort who'd be a
stranger anywhere.

21... M12S TONY MERVYN   MERVYN That's really why I came round
to see you Hancock. You're a man of
the world. An older man....
TONY   Not so much of the Old Mervyn.

22... MS TONY   More mature perhaps. I suppose I am
fortunate really. The world is my
oyster. I can be at home anywhere.
Fit in. Adapt myself to the customs
of the local natives. It's all down
to the old alma mater really. There you
are good grounding of Latin and Biology
and you can conquor the world.

23.. ML2S TONY MERVYN   MERVYN I knew you would supply
me with the inspiration I need.

TONY CROSSES TO POT PLANT
PUTS IT ON TABLE.   TONY You've got to have the strength
to cut the ties that bind - strick out
on your own - take the bit between
your teeth - stand on your own two
feet - put your nose to the grindstone

and always remember, he who hesitates
is lost.

TONY PULLS PLANT FROM POT COLLECTS
FLAG FROM SUITCASE, RETURNS TO TABLE.

24... CU FLAG IN POT OUT TO MS TONY
     SALUTING QUEEN VIC. PHOTOGRAPH.

25... MS TONY SALUTING

26... CU QUEEN VIC. PHOTOGRAPH

27... MS MERVYN SALUTING

28... L2S TONY MERVYN

TONY   At ease

MERVYN   Oh Hancock, I wish I had
your power of oratory.

29... M2S TONY MERVYN

TONY   It's hardly fair that one man
should have so much. Well Mervyn,
it's a bit late for education but
I could give you a crash course
in the bulldog spirit of independence.
You see the secret my friend is to
soak up the local culture as soon
as possible. Remember this country
has broken away from Mother England.
Is now standing on its own four feet
establishing a culture of its own
and this we must observe, and what
better way than through the most
modern means of mass communication
so far devised.

30... MS TONY OVER T.V.
     TONY SWITCHES SET ON PICKS
     UP PROGRAMME GUIDE AND SITS
     WITH MERVYN ON SETTEE.

TONY   Sit down, here we are. Here's
the indication of the local civilisation.
Now we'll find what makes these
people tick. READS   "Boom Town"
with Clark Gable and Spencer Tracy...
"The Three Stooges Meet Andy Hardy"..
Shirley Temple stars with Ronald
Reagan in "The Little General"...
The Marx Brothers in "Duck Soup"...
Faye Raye in "King Kon"...

31... CU TONY

See how this young colony has advanced.

        FADE OUT

end REEL 7

REEL 8

1... BILLBOARD

2... EST. SHOT

3... MS TONY

SCENE 23. TONY'S FLAT DAY LUNCHTIME

TONY IS SEATED ON THE SOFA. WATCHING
TELEVISION.

<u>VOICE</u>

And as they come to the last furlong
it's still Old Bill from My Kind of
Life and the rest very much out of it
at this stage. And George Moore's
letting Old Bill have his head.
He must win. He must win. Tony rises
but at the post it's My Kind of Life.
It's a sensational victory for My Kind
of Life.
TONY SWITCHES CHANNELS
<u>TONY</u>   Well it's not My Kind of Life
mate.
<u>VOICE</u>   And after that over from Tony
Lock it seems apparent to me Ritchie
that the wicket's not taking spin.
What would you say?
<u>VOICE</u>
Oh most definitely er Lindsay. Er It's
apparent that the er wicket is not
taking spin.
<u>TONY</u>   And I'm not taking any more of
that...

TONY SWITCHES CHANNELS   <u>VOICE</u>   And she's going on to win
yet another Open 1,500 metres
championship....
<u>VOICE</u>   Eight years Old Glenys
Plowright from Woolloomooloo doing
it again.

TONY SWITCHES OFF T.V.   <u>TONY</u>   Eight years old.

4... MCU TONY
eight years old what a place to live
in. They're all sport mad. Swimming
at eight years old? I hadn't had me
first <u>bath</u> at that age. There's no
escape from sport in this place, they're
at it from dawn to dusk. You can't
get any sense out of that infernal

PAN WITH HIM EASE OUT AS   machine. Let's see if there's anything
HE SITS LOOKS FOR PAPER.   in the newspapers. Lets see now an
wait a minute. Here we are. That's
more like it. Look at those headlines.
General Command Under Review...

5... MCU TONY
Old Monty's at it again eh? There's
no stopping him stirring them up in
Whitehall again. He'll never hang up
his beret. READS ALOUD General
Command under Review... What's this

New Zealand mare Review became
favourite over General Command for
the Eclipse Stakes.

6... MS TONY   Oh, it's all too much.
    HURLS PAPER DOWN.   What is a man to do? Here I am a
scholar, who can't carry on an
intellectual conversation unless I
go into full athletic training for
six months. They're bounding and
leaping and jumping about all over
the place. They stand still just so
long as it takes to get the result of
the last race. I came over here to
try to introduce a little culture.
I'm no Billy Graham.. My message needs
the intimacy of the Parisian Left
Bank Cage Society. And I don't go
much on all this wearing shorts in
Public. There's a time and place for
everything. What a man does in the
privacy of his own chambers is up to
him. But flaunting himself in public?
This depravity must cease...Well I
suppose old Dr. Livingstone had his
setbacks, Stanley for example. We
missionaries must persevere. Oh, if
only there was a mental Olympic Games..
I'll say one thing about all that

7... LS TONY AS HE RISES AND CROSSES
    TO KITCHEN EXITS SHOT   cavorting about it gives a man an
appetite.

8... CU SINK, LITTERED WITH AN
    ACCUMULATION OF UNWASHED DISHES.
    OUT TO MLS TONY LOOKS ROUND.   TONY   Ho, dear Oh dear I bet Errol
Flynn couldn't have hacked his way
through this lot single handed..

    IN TO MCU   I'll bet Godfrey Winn doesn't do
his own washing up either. Ah
decisions, decisions.

9... MS TONY CONFRONTED BY CEREAL
    PACKS IN F/G.   What shall it be Fruity Flakes energy
packed, vitamin enriched, as-eaten-
by world-Champions. Or perhaps soft
to .to the tongue, sun kissed Tasty
Pasties for Men? (POURS OUT ENERGY
PACKET) I can't see myself going
three rounds with Cassius Clay with
    A PLASTIC GIRAFFE FALLS   a bowl full of this stuff.
    ONTO HIS PLATE.

	Oh no, I've got the Giraffe again. I've got three of these already. Why
INTO MCU	can't I get the packet with the hippopotamus in? TCH OH.
10.. MLS	OPENS FRIDGE AND TAKES OUT NEW CARTON OF MILK - SMELLS CARTON That hasn't
HE TRIES TO OPEN THE CARTON	gone off.
	I'd like to have seen Houdini get out of one of these. He'd have curdled and turned into yoghurt.
READS INSTRUCTIONS	Now let's see... light blue touch paper and retire. No, no, no... pull here to form spout bend, hang on bend well back, pull apart.
P'N DOWN TO MILKY MESS.	HE PULLS WHOLE CARTON APART MILK SPILLS.
1.. SIDE MS TONY LOOKING DOWN AT SPILT MILK. PICKS UP LITTLE GIRAFFE.	TONY Tchh fat lotof use you are. Pity you weren't a cat...
PUSHES BOWL AWAY	Oh well I suppose this means another hard boild egg. TAKES EGG FROM FRIDGE. I dunno it's about time for a change.
12.. MCU TONY	I think I'll have it soft boiled. Now how do you cook a soft boiled egg? Funny how you get into a routine and it's hard to break. I bet Mrs. Beeton had the same trouble. Now where's my cook book?
13.. MLS TONY LOOK AT THIS. HE TAKES COOKERY BOOKS FROM SHELF, OPENS A COOK BOOK FULL OF NEWSPAPER CUTTINGS.	
14.. FRONTAL MS	TONY READS Lets see Oh - After yesterday's gruelling, action packed, bruising marathon at Dunstor Park it looks as if the Honourable Mildred Braithwaite will retain her World Championship Croquet title... (MUSING) She will, will she?
SLOW IN TO MCU	What on earth possessed me to keep that? TURNS CUTTING OVER Oh, it's on the back. Yes of course. Oh Pheasant Nureyev. Right take half a bottle of cognac, add a quarter bottle of drambuie and throw in some Kirsch. I don't know about the Pheasant, I think I'll settle for the gravy. No it's a bit heavy for this time of the day.

15₁. MLS TONY REFERS TO ANOTHER
   COOK BOOK   There must be something else you can
              do with eggs. Let's have a look at
   FLICKS THROUGH   Mrs. Beeton's book.
              Where are we, oh yes, egg nog -
              egg shampoo. I want a change but
              I'm not going to start a cooking
              revolution. Ah, hello, this looks
              within my means.

16.. MCU TONY TURNS TOWARD SINK Oeuf francaise.

17.. MS AS HE TAKES SAUCEPAN AND
   EMPTIES OUT WATER INTO SINK.

18.. MLS AS HE CROSSES TO B.BAR. First catch your egg.
   THROWS EGG UP AND CATCHES IT. Place egg in a seasoned saucepan to
              season saucepan take pinch of sea salt

19.. LS AS HE CROSSES KITCHEN FETCHES SALT

20.. MS AT B.BAR ADDS SALT

21.. LS HALF CROSSED K.

22.. MS AT B.BAR REFERS TO BOOK Add some oayenne peper

23.. MS AT SINK FETCHES PEPER

24.. MS AT B.BAR ADDS PEPPER   Formidable! A twist of vinegar.

25.. MS AT SINK FETCHES VINEGAR

26.. MS AT B.BAR   Just a soupcon..that was a good year..
              add water gently

27.. MS AT SINK ADDS WATER

28.. MS AT B.BAR   Bring to the boil

29.. LS   On a low overn.

30.. MS AT B.BAR   A low over. No I think I'll cheat I'll
              use the top.

31.. MS AT COOKER IN TO MCU   There's no doubt about the French,
              they may not be able to control their
              own destinies, but give them a bottle
              of cochineal and a cucumber and there's
              no holding them. Well, there's
              nothing else for it. I knew I had
              to face it sometime. Into the sink.

32.. CU TAPS TONY TURNS THEM ON.
   MOUNTAINS OF DIRTY DISHES BESIDE
   THE SINK. TONY TILLS IT WITH
   HOT WATER AND ADDS WASHING-UP
   LIQUID. HE PICKS UP DINNER PLATE
   SCATCHES IT AND SMELLS HIS FINGER.

            TONY Curry? Don't remember having
            curry. Must have been curried boiled
            egg.

   PUTS THE PLATE ON THEBACK OF
   HIS ELBOW JUGGLER-STYLE AND FLIPS
   IT UP AND BACK. DOES IT AGAIN
   MISSES.

33.. LS AS PLATE BREAKS

34,˙. MS REACTION	Ahem – yes.
35.. CU	I really should eat out more.
OUT TO MS	
TURNS TAP OFF HE POURS MORE DETERGENT IN – RUBS HANDS TOGETHER – LOOKS AT DETERGENT BOTTLE.	Musn't waste water.
	TONY New star detergent. Used by nine out of ten of Hollywood's stars. Ha ha ha I'd just like to see
36.. LS	John Wayne doing the washing up.
CROSSES TO COUNTER THEN BACK.	
37.. MS TONY DRAWS TWO IMAGINARY GUNS JOHN WAYNE – TYPE WALK TO SINK PLUNGING BOTH HANDS INTO HOT WATER.	TONY Ahhhh....
HE SEARCHES THROUGH DISHES TO FIND AND EGG CUP WHICH HE WASHES CAREFULLY DRIES ON TEA TOWEL AND LETS WATER OUT OF SINK, SWILLING IT ROUND WITH MORE WATER. THEN HE TAKES A TEA SPOON AND WITHOUT WASHING IT CLEANS IT ON TEA TOWEL.	
HE GOES TO BOILING SAUCEPAN SNIFS AT IT KNOWLEDGEABLY. DIPS SPOON IN AND TASTES THE WATER.	
38.. MCU	TONY Mmmmmmm. Just right.
39.. MLS TAKES WOODEN SPOON FISHES OUT EGG.	This egg sums it all up really. It's a matter of attitudes. In France this is a delicacy. Over here they'd turn this into a 100 yard race. A bit of chewing gum on the spoon. I bet they haven't rumbled that one!
EGG AND SPOON RACE TO COUNTER	
40.. MS HE PUTS EGG INTO CUP, AND SMASHES ITS SHELL WITH THE SPOON.	
IN TO CU	TONY It's just a hard boiled egg.

END REEL 8

41... BILLBOARD   MUSIC

COMMERCIAL   BREAK

REEL   9
42.. BILLBOARD   MUSIC

SCENE 23

43...CU TONY'S BACK HE WALKS TO DOOR
                    TONY Well that's enough exercise for
me for one day.

HOLD IN MLS   HE OPENS DOOR TO
THE MILKMAN.

LOOKS AT WATCH

MILKMAN   Morning   or should I say
afternoon.

TONY   What day is it?

MILKMAN   Saturday mate. Milk bill

HANDS TONY BILL.

TONY   Oh yes. Just a minute.

GOES IN SEARCH OF MONEY,
LEAVING MILKMAN AT DOOR.
SEARCHES JACKET FINDS CARD

What's this.

44..MCU

Owing to your behaviour at the party
last night, I'm changing my 'phone
number Max. Max? Never heard of him.

45..L.S. TONY MILKMAN PAN WITH TONY

MILKMAN   Hey, get a move on mate. The
big games's on this afternoon.

TONY   Yes I'll bet it is   Well you
can come and help with the big search,
'cos I can't find me money.

MILKMAN   (O.O.V.)   Oh yes?

TONY   No honestly. I'm the most
disorganised person on earth.

CROSSES TO MILKMAN   That's the trouble
with being an intellectual, your mind's
on bigger things.

MILKMAN

SLAPS TONY'S BELLY

You've got something big to think about
right there. What you need is a work
out.

46.. MS TONY

Take care of the body and the mind will
look after itself. I mean.. take a
good look at yourself.

TONY TAKES A LOOK AT HIMSELF AS IF DISCOVERING
HIMSELF ANEW.

TONY   Well I must admit it is some
time since I last broke the four
minutes...Long before Roger Bannister
thought about it of course.

MILKMAN   You're a miler?

TONY   Well no... but the fifty yard
dash to the bus stop, everybody said
I was very promising.

47... ML2S   TONY MILKMAN

MILKMAN   I keep myself in shape
running on my milk round. Why don't you
do what I do.

TONY   I have no intenetion my dear sir
of delivering milk at my time of life.

TONY CONTINUES SEARCH PAN
WITH HIM.

HE GOES TO CABINET.

now where could I have put that.
This is ridiculous, oh perhaps it's
in here.

48... MS TONY TAKES OUT SLICE OF
    BREAD.

Wait a minute I wonder what I put in
the toaster this morning?

49... L.S. TONY HE RETURNS

MILKMAN   (OOV)
You know what you need is a set routine
of exercises... It's all down to
regularity. Take five minutes a day
and before long you'll be as fit as I
am. You want to start with something
simple like skipping.

TAKES SASH FROM TONY'S DRESSING
GOWN.

50.. O.S. M2S FAVOURING TONY
    L.S. TONY MILKMAN
    MILKMAN STARTS SKIPPING

MILKMAN Get rid of me bag. Here
we go.
It's a great thing
TONY I'm sure it is (STILL LOOKING FOR
       MONEY)
The best thing I can do is to stop
drinking milk.
MILKMAN Here we go, you have a go

HANDS TONY SASH

now. Gently to start with, then a
few quick ones.
TONY Right
MILKMAN Hang on I'll get the bag out.

51.. M.S. TONY AS HE TRIES TO SKIP

TONY Funny isn't if like riding bike
after 20 years... you never quite lose
your touch. Just a minute.
(REMOVES GOWN)

52.. L.S.

TONY Hang on now then.
MILKMAN Do it to my count.
TONY Wait a minute - Right
MILKMAN Here we go.

53.. MLS TONY
    TONY BRINGS SASH OVER HIS
    HEAD. KNOCKS VASE OFF TABLE
    VASE SMASHES MONEY ROLLS OUT
54.. CU VASE   F/X

MILKMAN A - one.

55.. MS TONY

TONY I don't know me own strength
LOOKS AT BROKEN VASE That's one good
thing. At least I've found the money

PICKS UP SOME MONEY PAYS
MILKMAN.

Right that's that fixed up O.K. I
wont delay you any longer.
MILKMAN Ha. I'm just getting
warmed up. Come on now - running on
the spot. Up one, two three. Up one,
two three..

TONY UNWILLINGLY FALLS INTO
·RUNNING ON THE SPOT.
56.. MCU TONY

MILKMAN   I got these exercises
fromthe Royal Canadian Airforce
Manual.
TONY   (PUFFING)
You've just given me another reason
for hating flying.
MILKMAN   (OOV)
Oh don't be silly. These exercises
were thought up for men just like you.
How do you expect to win friends in
this country if you're not in peak
condition. A man here needs a sport.
TONY   Can I get by with Chess?
MILKMAN   Agh get yourself a real sport,
a good club and you're away.
TONY   (THOUGHTFULLY)
Yes, perhaps you're right. I could
infiltrate my own theories and turn
the whole nation over to my way of
thinking. (RUNNING ON THE SPOT STILL)
How many of these do you think I
ought to do?

57..LS TONY MILKMAN

MILKMAN You just keep that up till I
get back.
TONY   You won't be long. You will
come back?
MILKMAN   Yer. My crate's just
outside the door. What you could
do with is a real good workout on the
weights.

58..MS TONY

TONY   HOw Ron Clarke keeps up this
for three miles at a time I do not
know. And what's the point of it all?

59.. LS

MILKMAN   RETURNS WITH MILK CRATE
On your feet. On your feet.
TONY STAGGERS UP No slacking there.
That wasn't the spirit that won the
Battle of Britain, I bet.
TONY   Not so sure of that. They also
served who stood and stares.

EASE IN TO MLS
MILKMAN PUTS CRATE ON FLOOR
AND LIFTS IT BRISKLY FIST TO
WAIST HEIGHT THEN ABOVE HIS
HEAD, BREATHING EXPERTLY AND
COUNTING IN TIME.

MILKMAN   Here we go, One two, three,
four, five, six, seven, eight, nine,
ten....   THRUSTS CRATE AT TONY
Now you.

TONY TAKES CRATE WHICH TAKES HIM
BENDING TO THE FLOOR WITH ITS
WEIGHT.

60..MS TONY   TONY   STANDS
                                    Cor, deceptive things these milk crates
aren't they. Yes well, you'll be
wanting to get away to the match. I
s'pose.

61..MLS TONY MILKMAN   MILKMAN Yeah I suppose I had better be
going. Hey listen what are you
doing this afternoon.

62..MS TONY   TONY Oh just pondering over a few
equations, delve into Plato. a light
mental workout, nothing serious.

63..LS TONY MILKMAN   MILKMAN AH too much of that sort of
stuff and you'll go round the twist
Listen why don't you come down with

    EASE IN TO M2S   me and I'll show you how we spend a real
Australian sporting afternoon.
                                      TONY   I suppose a change of scene.
Get a bit of fresh air in me lungs,
And who knows, today could be the
start of an intellectual revolution.
'ang on, I'll just got a fling a few
clothes on.

HE MOVES TOWARDS BEDROOM SPARRING
LIKE A BOXER.

64.. BILLBOARD   MUSIC

COMMERCIAL BREAK

1..BILLBOARD   MUSIC
                                    SCENE 24   EXT DAY SYDNEY LEAGUES CLUB

2.. TONY MILKMAN WALK TO CLUB MUSIC
3.. REVERSE ANGLE PAN UP TO SIGN.

1.. TONY MILKMAN WALK TO BAR   SCENE 25 INT. LEAGUES CLUB BAR DAY.
2.. REVERSE ANGLE TONY MILKMAN
    ARRIVE AT BAR.   MILKMAN   Say fella's I'd like you to
meet Tony. That's Ken, Pete, Herbie and
Chips. (HELLOS) Tony's over from
England and I thought I'd show him
how we spend a Saturday afternoon.
                                    TONY   Of course you chaps are world
renowned as sportsmen.

3.. 3S TONY KEN PETE   KEN   Well it's only to be expected
what with all this sunshine and
nourishing food. Six schooners, love.
                                    TONY   (FUMBLING FOR MONEY)
Permit me....

PETE Ah put it away mate....

4... 2S HERB CHIPS HERBIE There'll be plenty of
opportunity for that later mate.

CHIPS (CLAPS HANDS)
Well well, who's going to win the big
one this afternoon mates.

5.. MCU TONY TONY SARCASTICALLY Which one d'you
mean the racing, the cricket, the
football, the tennis, the swimming,
the surfing or the trampoline?

6.. M2S TONY MILKMAN MILKMAN You've got a wider knowledge
of sport than I thought.

TONY Well I like to keep up with
television... and read the news papers.

7.. WS GROUP DRINKS ARE SERVED.
THANK YOU'S TA'S. MILKMAN Bet you don't get beer like
this where you come from.

TONY You can say that again.

MILKMAN Well chaps here's to the
mighty blues.

8.. MCU TONY THE REST Eat them alive.

TONY May the best team win.

9.. MCU CHIPS

10. MCU PETE

11. MCU HERB

12. MCU KEN

13. MCU TONY SIPPING DRINK

14. MCU HERB DOWNING HIS IN ONE GO HERB Same again, love.

15. 2S TONY MILKMAN TONY That was very nice. Very nice
indeed. LOOKS AT WATCH Well I suppose
they'll all be getting ready to punish
the leather spheroid....
How far's the ground from here?

MILKMAN It's only about half a mile
down the road.

TONY Oh we'd better get a cab then.

MILKMAN What for?

TONY The match.

MILKMAN Ha ha mmm we're not goin'
there.

TONY Well what's all this business
about fresh air in me lungs.

MILKMAN This place is air conditioned

MORE SCHOONERS SERVED. TONY
HAD NO IDEA THAT THIS WAS WHAT
HE WAS IN FOR - LOOKS BEWILDERED.

TONY Well what's all this talk
about physical fitness?

MILKMAN You're talking to some of the
best developed biceps men in the busine

16.. CU ARM DOWNING SCHOONER FOCUS
    ON TONY

17.. 3S TONY MILKMAN PETS   ALL   Cheers, cheers.

                              PETE   Don't suppose you English blokes
                              get much of a chance to play
                              sport, huh?

                              MILKMAN He said he was a four minuter.

18...MCU HERB   HERBIE Get a few pounds off him and
                              he would have made a good forward.

19.. MCU TONY   TONY   What do you mean would.
                              There're wern't many people who would
                              tangle with me. Ah it brings it all
                              back. The roar of the crowd, the
                              sting of the linament, the nervous
                              tension as you led the team onto
                              the field....

      DISSOLVE TO......

                              SCENE 26 RUGBY LEAGUE GROUND EXT. DAY

TONY LEADS A FULL TEAM OUT OF THE TUNNERL
ONTO AND ACROSS THE PITCH CROWDS CHEER
HE SHAKES HANDS WITH THE OPPOSING
CAPTAIN THEN HE SPINS COIN SIGNALS
TEAM TO CHANGE ENDS. TURNS AND RUNS
OFF, BACK INTO TUNNEL.

                              SCENE 27   LEAGUES CLUB BAR INT. DAY

1...CU TONY'S THUMB

    OUT TO MS TONY   TONY (SHOWING DOUBLE JOINTED THUMB)

                              Course I have tossed for England that
                              year if I hadn't dislocated me thumb.

    OUT TO INCLUDE PETE   PETE Yeah, well I'm a racing man
                              myself.

                              TONY Of course, the sport of Kings.

2..3S   PETE STANDS My father wanted me
                              to be a jockey, but I couldn't make
                              the weight.

3.. CU TONY   TONY   I never found it a handicap.

4.. 2S   PETE Were you a gentleman rider?

5.. CU TONY   TONY Well, I certainly wasn't a lady
                              rider....(LAUGHS)

6.. 2S   PETE (ASTONISED)
                              Are you sure about the weight? Did
                            you get many rides?
                            TONY I was in constant demand man
                            an owner was prepared to sacrifice
                            a few pounds to get a rider of my
                            calibre. When you're bidding for the

Blue Ribands of the turf a stone
here or there is a small price to pay.
PETE: Gee I would have loved to
have seen you in a race.
TONY   You should have been there.
Royal Ascot. The bookies shouting
the odds, the ladies in their hats
wishing me bon chance, the dramatic
hush as we were placed in the
starter's hands.

DISSOLVE TO   SCENE 28   RACECOURSE EXT. DAY

EST. SHOTS RACE COURSE TONY
ON HORSE ENTERS STARTING STALLS.
RACE STARTS, HORSES LEAVE MAN
WITH BINOCULARS LOOKS SHOTS OF
RACE. TONY URGING HORSE
ZOOM OUT REVEALS TONY STANDING
IN STALL SANS HORSE.   SCENE 29   LEAGUES CLUB BAR INT. DAY.

1... MS TONY   I thought I might have a go at the
                                       Melbourne Cup while I was out here.
                                       But for the life of me, I can't find
                                       me whip.

2... MS CHIPS   CHIPS   Being English I suppose you'd
                                       play more refined sports, like Polo..

3... MS TONY   TONY   I was forced into an early
                                       retirement. It was either that or the
                                       Tower. He's a poor loser, you know.
                                       CHIPS   Yeah well I can understand that

                             END REEL 9

                             REEL   10

                                       But there's plenty of other sports for
                                       the aristocrat.

4... CU TONY   TONY   Oh, yes, yes...
                                       CHIPS   What other sports did you pla,
                                       TONY   Well I had a bash at...er...
                                       What's that game called where you hit
                                       a ball at another ball and....

5... M2S TONY MILKMAN   MILKMAN   Golf?
                                       TONY   Golf that's right yes Royal
                                       and Ancient ha, ha ha Couldn't keep
                                       me away, rain or sun. Knew that course
                                       like the back of my hand. LOOKS AT
                                       HAND. It was the British Open of '58
                                       or was it '59 ah there were so many of
                                       them........

6... CU HAND PULLING BEER   BEERS PULLED   MUSIC. ....

SCENE 30   LEAGUES CLUB BAR. INT. DAY.

1...   4S   GROUP

CHIPS   My word there's a lot of
money to be picked up in big time golf

2...   CU   TONY
ALL HAVE ANOTHER ROUND OF
DRINKS IN THEIR HANDS.

TONY   You're right   Ten bob a round
plus tips.

3...   4S   GROUP

PETE   Cheers.....

REST   Cheers

4...   MS   HERBIE

HERBIE   All that rubbish about big
time sport. Being a jockey and
playing golf.... Some athlete you
are. You even put your glass down
between drinks.

5... MS TONY INCLUDING THUMB.

TONY   That's on account of my thumb.
You see that DEMONSTRATES AGAIN
Harold Larwood did that. In a game
of French Cricket for charity.

HERBIE   Oh I thought you got that
playing football?

TONY   I trust you're not picking
on a man's disabilities to ridicule
him?

6... MCU HERBIE

HERBIE   Not when there's so much
else to pick on.

7... MCU   TONY

TONY   Well of course there's little
to pick on at all. In fact there's
hardly anything of you... which in
a way is a blessing to mankind.....

8... 3S

HERBIE   Oh yer...

TONY   Yer...TO MILKMAN Look you'd
better stop him. He's heading
straight for a punch up the bracket.

MILKMAN   Herbie can take care of
himself all right. He was amateur
bantam weight champion.

TONY   They're always 'was'...

9...LS GROUP

HERBIE   STARTING TO SHAPE UP
I haven't forgotten how, mate...

TONY REACTS FIRST WITH BRAVADO AND
THEN SLIGHT COWARDICE. THE GROUP
SPLIT. KEN AND CHIPS BEHIND
TONY THE OTHERS BEHIND HERBIE.
TONY FORCES HIMSELF BACK WITH
HIS ARMS OUT.

10..3S
THE TWO MEN BEHIND HERBIE ARE
PHYSICALLY HOLDING HIM BACK.

TONY   Hold me back, hold me back,
before I do some damage.

11..3S HERBIES GROUP	HERBIE Let me go. Let me go. I'll kill him.
12..LS GROUP	TONY Cur.. you bounder... cad (BACKS AGAIN) Let me at him.
TONY BREAKS AWAY FROM GROUP BY MISTAKE FINDS HIMSELF FACE TO FACE WITH HERBIE REALISES HE IS FREE AND HURRIEDLY THROWS HIM-SELF BACK INTO HIS GROUP.	BARMAID All right. Come, on come on. Herbie, you should know better. You'd kill him.
13..CU TONY	TONY What? When I went in against Sugar Ray Robinson....
14..CU HERBIE	HERBIE There he goes again.
15..3S TONY'S GROUP	TONY Yer....
16..3S HERBIE'S GROUP	HERBIE Yer...
17..MS BARMAID	BARMAID If you're not careful you'll have another fight on your hands - with me. Nobody's paid for the last round o of drinks yet...

              FAD OUT)

                 FADE IN   SCENE 31   INT. DAY TONY'S FLAT

    EXT. EST. SHOT TONY'S FLAT

1...CU BALLET DANCER FOCUS ON TONY ON SOFA IN SIMILAR POSITION. HE IS READING "NEW SCIENTIST" THROWS IT DOWN COMES TO T.V. SWITCHES IT ON RETURNS TO SOFA.	T.V. VOICE Many of you may have missed the replay of yesterday's big game. so here's the Match of the Day from the Sports Stadium.
2.. CU TONY	
3.. MLS TONY SWITCHES OFF T.V.	TONY Oh no. I went through all that yesterday that's the sort of day I never want to go through again.
4.. MS TONY	I never want to hear about racehorses, tiddly winks or bosing kangaroos as long as I live. I'd prefer to stay
PAN L WITH HIM	a 97 pound weakling.... It's the mind, not muscles, that really matter in this world. Socrates, Plato Aristotle, they didn't play for the All Blacks. We're cast in the same mould. The only difference between us really is that they wore a sheet and I wear a dressing gown. They had no trouble making friends, they always had an eager group of students at their feet as they read out their latest

theories. Yes, that's what I need --
my own discussion group. I can see
it now, The Hancock Set. Perhaps a
few of my works hand printed. A forum
of prose and poetry. I'll ask round
Patrick White, Sid Nolan. In fact the
whole of Australian culture. That's
the best of being intelligent.

5...L.S. CROSSES TO BREAKFAST BAR   You can learn from your mistakes...
yes. I'll find a good literary
society. I could infiltrate my
own theories and turn the whole nation
over to my way of thinking. Let's

LOOKS THRU PHONE BOOK   see now wait a minute. .CI.T.Y.
CREEP IN TO M.S.
DIALS NUMBER   That's it this is more me The City
Arts Discussion Group.
Hello Yes This is Anthony Hancock.
I'd like to pop round to your Society
this afternoon for a quick soiree
rub shoulders with people like
shelly, Keats, Byron, Browning, it'll
be good to be back among old friends.
What? That is the City Arts Discussion
Group? No meeting today. Why

INCREDULOUS. HE CAN'T BELIEVE   not, in heaven's name?
ANSWER.
They've all gone to the football...
CU. TONY.

        FADE OUT BILLBOARD............

EPILOGUE

It Was a Cold Day Suddenly

On the day after Tony's death, Clare Richardson wrote to her parents in England: 'I returned to ATN. Such is the nature of the human animal that probably the chief emotion was one of gratification that the most coveted top production of the station had been removed from our team's hands. Being the only member of the team who was there at the time, I was almost completely ignored. No sympathy was extended to me, no kind words spoken. Of course people were embarrassed as well and I fully understood that none of it was caused by a personal dislike of me, but it was a cold day suddenly, with nothing to do.'

Tony's death heralded my demotion. My plush office at ATN-7 – known as the best seat in the house – which the chairman visited maybe two days a year, became needed 'on a regular basis,' or so I was informed when I went to the studio a few days later. All my files and belongings had been moved from the airy, spacious, luxuriously furnished office to which I had speedily grown accustomed, to a tiny, scruffy, stuffy, airless, windowless, storeroom at the end of a long, dimly lit basement corridor. I had to share this claustrophobic corner with an elderly ATN-7 staff director who, having passed his sell-by date, had also been banished to this Sydney Siberia. I remembered the recycled Kenny More head at the waxworks and wondered when the rats would reach our dungeon.

A Sydney newspaper guesstimated that ATN-7 lost over \$A100,000 on the Hancock series. This is a very conservative figure, considerably below the real cost. But even at today's rates that 100K would be in the region of half a million quid. ATN-7's ratings were starting to nose dive thanks to the recent introduction of a third Sydney based commercial television station whose atrocious programmes were so excruciatingly awful that they became cult viewing. Accordingly Channel 7's advertising was adversely affected and every cent saved was a cent earned so I can't blame them for their parsimonious behaviour relating to money spent on completing the Hancock Special and the King's Cross documentary both of which I continued to work on as and when my editor and film crew were not assigned to other, more important, ATN-7 productions.

This left me a lot of spare time which I filled in by making an independent film for ITV in the UK about the so-called Ten Pound Migrants to Australia as seen through the eyes of a family who'd been settled there for 20 years, contrasting their experiences with those of a newly arrived couple with a young baby. I didn't make a fortune out of it, but sufficient to pay cash for a new car. A small car mind.

So, what about the other dramatis personae in this Australian drama?

Clare Richardson took off for the Great Barrier Reef. Mike Wale flew to England and Hugh Stuckey went home to Melbourne. Surprise, surprise, Hugh never did get the verbal commission he'd been offered for a further 13 shows. Dusty Nelson was a staff man so he was OK.

My wife had become an overnight success in Sydney. Casting director Franz Conde, on the lookout for artistes to sign up to start his own talent agency, auditioned my wife. He flipped when she sang him some spontaneous topical ditties about news events in Oz. As she could write lyrics and music in minutes, he immediately signed her for a new variety/talk series which ATN-7 was launching. She adopted the stage name of Merlyn, and sang the weekly news – along the lines of Millie Martin's efforts in *That Was The Week That Was*. Within weeks she was a celebrity, guesting on most of ATN-7's talk shows and panel games and appearing at Sydney night clubs singing and playing her guitar.

212

ATN-7 seconded me to Artransa Film Productions to advise them on new projects, after which they wanted me to work on a local light entertainment series. I felt the latter would be a retrograde move because of some encouraging noises from International Artistes. As nothing more challenging was on offer, I returned to the UK where I had a job waiting for me. My children stayed in Sydney with my wife until her contracts were fulfilled and then they too returned to the UK.

It wasn't easy for Merlyn to revert to being a housewife and a mum after savouring the heady delights of stardom Down Under. Our marriage wasn't working and we parted.

But that's another story.

BIBLIOGRAPHY

John Freeman, *Face to Face*, Jonathan Cape, 1964

Ray Galton and Alan Simpson, *Hancock* (Four Scripts), Andre Deutsch, 1961

Ray Galton and Alan Simpson, *The Rebel*, Alan Holmes Adaptation, Mayfair Books, 1961

Ray Galton and Alan Simpson, *Hancock's Half Hour*, The Woburn Press, 1974

Ray Galton and Alan Simpson, *The Best of Hancock*, Robson, 1986

Ray Galton and Alan Simpson, Hancock's Half Hour – The Classic Years, BBC, 1987

Cliff Goodwin, *Sid James*, Century, 1995

Joan Le Mesurier, *Lady Don't Fall Backwards*, Sidgwick & Jackson, 1988; Pan Books, 1989

John Le Mesurier, *A Jobbing Actor*, Elm Tree Books, 1984; Sphere Books, 1985

Phillip Oakes, *The Entertainers – Tony Hancock*, The Woburn Press, 1975

Freddie Ross and David Nathan, *Hancock*, William Kimber & Co. Ltd., 1969; Coronet, 1975

Heathcote Williams, *Hancock's Last Half Hour*, Polantic Press, 1977

Roger Wilmut, *Tony Hancock Artiste*, Eyre Methuen, 1978

Roger Wilmut, *The Illustrated Hancock*, Queen Anne Press, 1986

INDEX

217

218